CONTENTS

Ships in Focus Publications

Correspondence and editorial:
Roy Fenton
18 Durrington Avenue
London SW20 8NT
0181 879 3527
rfenton@rfenton.demon.co.uk
Orders and photographic:
John & Marion Clarkson
18 Franklands, Longton
Preston PR4 5PD
01772 612855

Printed by Amadeus Press Ltd.,
Huddersfield.
Designed by Hugh Smallwood, John
Clarkson and Roy Fenton.
SHIPS IN FOCUS RECORD
ISBN 0 901703 06 1

SHIPS IN FOCUS RECORD 10

No editor likes raising the s[?]
money is necessary to ma[?]
specialist magazine is cost[?]
editorial time. As loyal read[?]
the help of Amadeus Pr[?]
photographic reproduction. [?]
authors. And behind the sce[?]
ensure our photographic cov[?] [?]
our facts are accurate, that articles are carefully edited and proof
read, and that *all* correspondents and contributors get a prompt
reply. All this takes time and money, so - as you will no doubt have
guessed - we are having to increase the cover price of *Record*. With
effect from the next issue, number 11 due in February 2000, it will
cost £7.

However - and here's the good news - we are also
offering readers a way to avoid the price increase: take out a
subscription or extend your existing one. A subscription for one or
two years will bring you *Record* at the bargain prices shown below.
For instance, a UK subscriber taking out a two year subscription,
will save £8, a European subscriber £10. If your existing
subscription has still some time to run, you are welcome to extend
it up to a total of two years. Subscribers also benefit from offers on
other *Ships in Focus* publications, like our forthcoming *Burns and
Laird* announced opposite.

But whether or not you subscribe, we hope you continue
to read *Record,* and what we firmly believe is the best value in
illustrated shipping history. For our part, we promise to continue
to provide an expanding range of high-quality photographic and
written contributions. This issue, for instance, sees us take an in-
depth look at the career of a well-loved coastal passenger ship,
provide a photographic history of a small but significant cargo liner
fleet, and commemorate the start of the disastrous Boer War with a
look at some of the transports involved. *Record* 11 is well
advanced, and will include cargo liners, the work of a well-known
1950s photographer, tugs, coasters, Clyde passenger ships, and
much more. We hope you'll join us.

John Clarkson   Roy Fenton
October 1999

SUBSCRIPTION RATES FOR THREE ISSUES OF RECORD
Subscribers make a saving on the postage of three issues, and receive
each *Record* just as soon as it is published. They are also eligible for
concessions on newly-published *Ships in Focus* titles. Readers can
start their subscription with *any* issue, and are welcome to backdate it
to receive previous issues.

	One year (3 issues)	Two years (6 issues)
UK	£20	£40
Europe (airmail)	£22	£44
Rest of world (surface mail)	£22 or US$36	£44 or US$72
Rest of world (airmail)	£30 or US$49	£60 or US$98

JONATHAN HOLT (3): see page 73. *[Geoffrey Holmes collection]*

The Cammell Laird-built ROBERT L. HOLT (2) of 1946 spent her entire life with John Holt and the Guinea Gulf Line. *[Fotoflite incorporating Skyfotos]*

Fleet in Focus
JOHN HOLT
Geoffrey Holmes

In July 1862 the twenty-year old John Holt arrived at Santa Isabel, Fernando Po, to take up the post of secretary to a merchant who was also the British Consul on the island. Two years later his employer died and Holt became the sole manager of the business which he eventually bought outright in April 1867. His two brothers joined the business and in 1868 the eldest, Jonathan, returned to England and obtained his master's certificate. He then purchased, on behalf of John Holt, the schooner MARIA which he sailed out to Fernando Po. Over the next seventeen years the business expanded on to the West African mainland in the Cameroons, Spanish Guinea and Gabon, with a Liverpool office being established in 1874. Jonathan Holt was taken into partnership in 1884 - the company title becoming John Holt and Co. In March 1897, following Jonathan's death in the previous year, a limited company was established under the title John Holt and Co. (Liverpool) Ltd. By this time Holts were established traders throughout the Bight of Benin, the Niger Delta and southward to Angola and the French and Belgian Congo.

Ocean-going steamers

Whilst Holts had owned schooners and one small steamship which traded along the West African coast and into the Niger delta, it was not until 1907 that the company acquired its first ocean going steamship - the BALMORE. Three years later two steamers were ordered: JONATHAN HOLT and THOMAS HOLT. These ships were fitted out to company specification and were the first in the West African trade to be fitted with mosquito screens to ports, windows and doors. John Holt was one of the founders of the Liverpool School of Tropical Medicine and these anti-mosquito precautions were at the suggestion of Major Ronald Ross (later Sir Ronald) who had discovered that the female mosquito was the source of malarial infection. The wartime loss of the JONATHAN HOLT and then the USSA, acquired as her replacement, necessitated the purchase of the CLEMATIS in 1920. The BALMORE was sold in 1922 and, for the next four years the service was maintained by just two ships - THOMAS HOLT (1) and CLEMATIS.

During the late nineteen twenties new vessels entered service which, after disposal of older tonnage, brought the fleet up to five ships. Until 1939 a regular service was maintained from north west Brunswick Dock, Liverpool, to Takoradi, Accra, Lome, Cotonou, Lagos, Port Harcourt, Victoria, Douala and terminating at Warri. Holts had become established at Warri in 1900 and a fleet of river craft was built up which traded for some 900 miles up the Niger and its tributary the Benue.

War service

On the outbreak of war in 1939 the ocean-going fleet comprised five ships. Losses were heavy with only two of the pre-war fleet surviving. In addition, the third JOHN HOLT was lost after less than twelve months in service. Two of the ships assisted in evacuating troops from St. Nazaire in June 1940 with the JOHN HOLT (2) picking up 1,100 survivors from the LANCASTRIA and landing them at Plymouth. The ROBERT L. HOLT was lost with all hands and there was also heavy loss of life when both the JONATHAN HOLT (2) and the JOHN HOLT (3) were sunk. Replacement tonnage was ordered in 1945 which restored the fleet to five ships.

Trade and terminals

Warri was still a major centre of operations with the company's river fleet being based there. A slipway and engineering workshops for this fleet were maintained as well as warehouses and deep-water jetties. The river fleet was sold in 1949 but remained under Holts' management. A new concrete wharf was built in 1961 and the FLORENCE HOLT took part in the opening ceremony.

During the war the fleet had been common carriers under the Liner Requisition Scheme. This arrangement continued after the war and in 1950 the company decided that shipping should be separated from the group's other business and the John Holt Line Ltd. was established on 1st January 1950. The United Africa Company established Palm Line at the same time and for the same reason. The new company joined the West African Lines Conference - WALCON. This meant that the ships were now also to be seen on the east coast of the UK and in Continental ports. On 11th January 1954 the company name was changed to the Guinea Gulf Line Ltd. The increasing co-operation between the three British-flag carriers on the West African trade led to an amalgamation of the companies' stevedoring at Tilbury in November 1955 under the name West African Terminals. In July 1961 a similar amalgamation took place at Liverpool (Liverpool West African Terminals).

Post-war renewal

In 1951 the surviving pre-war ships, THOMAS HOLT (2) and GODFREY B. HOLT, were sold and two new vessels ordered. The ELIZABETH HOLT and her sister FLORENCE HOLT were considerably bigger than previous tonnage and were the company's first turbine steamers. Further additions were made to the fleet at the end of the fifties with the ROSE OF LANCASTER and the MARY HOLT coming from Grays of West Hartlepool. This brought the fleet up to seven ships and, in addition, chartered vessels were used. The KEPWICKHALL of the West Hartlepool Navigation Co. Ltd. made several voyages around 1961. The ROSE OF LANCASTER was bareboat chartered from her Bermudan owners, Red Rose Navigation Co. Ltd., who were, in turn, a subsidiary of the Guinea Gulf Line. This vessel was registered in Liverpool and manned by Guinea Gulf personnel. The only difference to the other ships was that she flew the Red Rose houseflag in addition to that of Guinea Gulf. The ships were to be seen in most ports along the West African Coast from Dakar to the Congo and occasionally Angola. Most of the cargo was carried to and from Nigeria and Ghana. UK and Continental ports were also served.

Outward the ships carried general cargo. Homeward, the cargo mainly consisted of bagged produce - palm kernels and ground nuts - together with logs, plywood and sawn timber. Logs were usually between three and five tons when they were launched into the water but, by the time they were loaded, the weight was considerably in excess of this due to absorption of water. As a result, a 10-ton derrick was usually needed to load them. Many logs were much heavier and required the use of the heavy lift derrick: the heaviest log the author saw loaded weighed 43 tons. Palm oil was also carried and the newer ships had deep tanks for this cargo.

The Kru boys and surf ports

In the autumn of 1960 Nigeria gained independence, bringing a number of changes for the companies trading to that country. Like the other British lines - Elder Dempster and Palm Line - it had been the custom for Holts' ships to pick up their own labour at either Freetown or, more usually, Takoradi. Known as Kru boys, these labourers slept on number 1 hatch under a canopy rigged from the hatch derricks which were topped. There were cabins and a galley in the forecastle for their use. Rations were drawn from the ship. All the cargo work along the coast was performed by these labourers as well as general maintenance under the direction of the boatswain. However, the new Nigerian government insisted that local labour be used. Nigerian labourers were carried for a short period but the custom ceased as the various ports built up their own labour forces.

The Kru boys came into their own at the surf ports along the West African coast: Cape Palmas, Accra, Cape Coast, Winneba, Keta, Lome, Cotonou and Victoria being the last survivors. Cargo was discharged on to surf boats or lighters. Some of these were only some 25 feet long and were paddled ashore. The ships would be rolling in the South Atlantic swell and it was a fine art to land the sling of cargo on the boat so as not to capsize it. Heavier items were handled by lashing two surf boats together. Some cargo inevitably ended up in the sea. The ships were provided with books of lost-overboard certificates which had to be completed by the duty mate when this occurred. By 1962 nearly all of these ports had been replaced by protected harbours such as that at Tema.

Outmoded

By the end of the 1950s the Guinea Gulf Line were feeling the effects of their policy of building steamers. Whilst the other companies in the trade were operating motor ships, Guinea Gulf had only steamers, and their three oldest were of a very outmoded design, having wooden hatch covers and small capacity derricks, some with rope topping lifts. The newer vessels had more modern cargo gear but, being steamers, were expensive to operate. The ships had been known as the Liverpool Yachts but the effect of an economy drive introduced at this time meant that standards slipped.

In September 1962 it was decided to place the ships under the management of T. and J. Brocklebank. The oldest ships were not included in this scheme. The JONATHAN HOLT (3) had already been sold whilst on an outward voyage and was delivered to her new owners at Lagos. A new subsidiary, Holts' Maritime Trading, was established to manage the JOHN HOLT (4) and ROBERT L. HOLT (2). It was intended that these two vessels would trade as tramps. The JOHN HOLT (4) was undergoing her fourth special survey in Liverpool and on completion of this she went to Barrow-in-Furness to lay up, arriving in Devonshire Dock on 2nd August 1962. The ROBERT L. HOLT (2) did make one tramping voyage, but on arriving at Calais to discharge it was found that her windlass bedplate was cracked. The cost of repair was considered to be uneconomic and she was sold for breaking up. JOHN HOLT (4) was sold in 1963.

During 1962 it was found that the Guinea Gulf Line had temporarily exceeded their share of conference tonnage. As a result the ELIZABETH HOLT was chartered to Brocklebanks and made a round voyage to India and Pakistan arriving back in the UK in January 1963. In the autumn of 1963 Brocklebanks' MASKELIYA made a round voyage to West Africa for Guinea Gulf. Both vessels carried the charterer's funnel colours on these voyages.

The company sold

During 1964 protracted negotiations took place with the Nigerian Government with a view to selling the company to the Nigerian National Line. These negotiations were fruitless and on 1st March 1965 the Guinea Gulf Line together with its four remaining ships was sold to Liner Holdings - the parent company of Elder Dempster Lines.

Except for the MARY HOLT, the four ships did not trade to West Africa after the sale. The MARY HOLT made one round voyage under Elder Dempster management before being sold to the National Shipping Corporation of Pakistan. Elder Dempster, after selling the Guinea Gulf steam ships, transferred six of their older motorships to their new subsidiary to maintain the Guinea Gulf share of the conference. In 1978 the last survivor of the old ships, the former ROSE OF LANCASTER, was broken up at Split.

John Holt and Co. (Liverpool) Ltd. had extensive interests beyond shipping. The Guinea Gulf agent in Freetown in the 1960s was employed by the local Ford dealer! The group were general traders and merchants throughout most of West Africa and there were also an insurance company, interests in the liquor trade in the UK and extensive vineyards in the Bordeaux region. The group was eventually absorbed by the conglomerate, Lonrho.

Fleet list of ocean-going ships

John Holt and Co. 1884-1897
John Holt and Co. (Liverpool) Ltd. 1897-1950
John Holt Line Ltd. 1950-1954
Guinea Gulf Line Ltd. 1954-1965

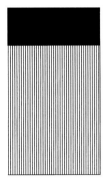 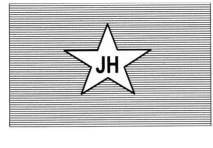

Flag and funnel used by John Holt and Co. 1884-1954. *[J.L. Loughran]*

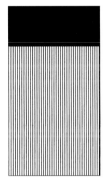 

Flag and funnel of Guinea Gulf Line Ltd. 1954-1965. *[J.L. Loughran]*

1. BALMORE 1907-1922
O.N. 96414   1,272g 783 n   229.0 x 32.5 x 16.1 feet
T. 3-cyl. by North Eastern Marine Engineering Co. Ltd., Newcastle-upon-Tyne.
9.1890: Completed by Thomas and William Smith, North Shields (Yard No. 102) for the Albany Shipping Co. Ltd. (David Scott and Son, managers), Dundee as BALMORE.
15.10.1907: Acquired by John Holt and Co. (Liverpool) Ltd., Liverpool.
11.1922: Sold to W. Biesterfeld Reederei und Schiff. G.m.b.H., Hamburg, Germany.

9.3.1923: Registered in Hamburg as JOHANNES TIEMANN.
9.12.1924: Sold to W. Schuchmann, Geestemünde, Germany.
25.1.1925: Renamed HOCHSEE.
10.1.1929: Sold to Litauische Schiffahrt und Handelsgesellschaft 'Lietgar' Klaipeda, Lithuania (W. Schuchmann, Geestemünde, manager) and renamed KLAIPEDA.
1929: Owners became Lietuvos Garlaiviy ir Prekybos Akeine B-ve. 'Lietgar', Klaipeda, Lithuania (W. Schuchmann, Bremerhaven, manager).
19.12.1931: Laid up at Bremerhaven.
22.3.1935: Owner became W. Schuchmann, Bremerhaven and renamed NORDSEE
4.12.1935: Sold for breaking up to Leth and Co., Hamburg.
1936: Sold to the Cadogan Steamship Co. Ltd. (T. Dunlop and Sons), Glasgow. She was bought in order to be scrapped under the British 'Scrap and Build' scheme to obtain part of a loan to build the motorship QUEEN ANNE (4,937/1937), but was never registered in the United Kingdom.
12.1936: Sold to A. Ritscher, Hamburg-Moorburg, Germany for breaking up.

2. JONATHAN HOLT (1)   1910-1917
O.N. 131274   1,522g 842n   251.1 x 38.0 x 16.1 feet.
T.3-cyl. by David Rowan and Co., Glasgow.
6.1910: Completed by William Hamilton and Co. Ltd., Port Glasgow (Yard No. 216) for John Holt and Co. (Liverpool) Ltd., Liverpool.
7.6.1917: Torpedoed by the German submarine U 54 130 miles north west by half west of Fastnet in position 51.24 north by 14.10 west whilst on a voyage from Sierra Leone to Liverpool with a cargo of palm oil and kernels.

3. THOMAS HOLT (1)/GARTHORPE (1)   1910-1929
O.N. 131283   1,522g 841n   251.0 x 38.0 x 16.1 feet
T. 3-cyl. by David Rowan and Co., Glasgow.
8. 1910: Completed by William Hamilton and Co. Ltd., Port Glasgow (Yard No. 217) for John Holt and Co. (Liverpool) Ltd., Liverpool as THOMAS HOLT.
1928: Renamed GARTHORPE.
12.1929: Sold to Bugsier Reederei und Bergungs A.G., Hamburg, Germany and renamed EILENAU.
4.3.1941: Sunk by gunfire from British destroyers including HMS TARTAR at Svolvær, Lofoten Islands during Operation Claymore.
1948: Refloated by Norsk Bjergningskompagni A/S, Bergen, Norway.
2.8.1951: Arrived at Antwerp from Bergen.
12.8.1951: Sold to V.F. van Loo.
9.1951: Broken up.

Holts' first order for new ships was for two steamers from William Hamilton at Port Glasgow which were delivered in 1910. First was JONATHAN HOLT (1), a First World War loss, of which no photographs have been found. This is the second, THOMAS HOLT (1). The split superstructure with the long bridge was perpetuated in the next group of new ships.

4. USSA 1916-1917

O.N. 135457 2,066g 1,077n 304.6 x 44.7 x 17.2 feet
T. 3-cyl. by the Clyde Shipbuilding and Engineering Co. Ltd., Port Glasgow.

5.1913: Completed by the Clyde Shipbuilding and Engineering Co. Ltd., Port Glasgow (Yard No. 303) for Stott (Baltic) Steamers Ltd. (W.H. Stott and Co. Ltd., managers), Liverpool as USSA.

20.4.1914: Sold to R. Martens and Co. Ltd., London.

28.6.1916: Acquired by John Holt and Co. (Liverpool) Ltd., Liverpool.

3.5.1917: Mined and sunk two and a half miles north west of the west entrance to Cherbourg Harbour whilst on a voyage from Manchester to Cherbourg with a cargo of hay and wagons. The mine had been laid earlier that day by the German submarine UC 26.

5. CLEMATIS 1920-1926

O.N. 109887 3,406g 2,161n 344.5 x 46.0 x 16.8 feet
T. 3-cyl. by the North Eastern Marine Engineering Co. Ltd., Newcastle-upon-Tyne.

18.6.1898: Launched by the Tyne Iron Shipbuilding Co. Ltd., Willington Quay-on-Tyne (Yard No. 120) for Stag Line Ltd. (Joseph Robinson and Sons, managers), North Shields as CLEMATIS.

7.1898: Completed.

2.5. 1916: Sold to Leeston Shipping Co. Ltd., Cardiff.

11.6.1920: Acquired by John Holt and Co. (Liverpool) Ltd., Liverpool.

9.1926: Sold to Società Anonima Marittima Catanese (G. Napoli e Figli, managers), Catania, Italy.

1929: Sold to shipbreakers at Catania, Italy.

Right: Depicted in the painting in the colours' of original owner Stag Line, CLEMATIS of 1898 was bought by John Holt without change of name in 1920. *[World Ship Photo Library]*

Below: JOHN HOLT (1) was the first of three ships delivered by Smith's Dock in 1926, clearly developments of the 1910 pair: note the extended bridge.

6. JOHN HOLT (1)/**GARTHORPE** (2) 1926-1939

O.N. 147352 2,909g 1,687n 310.0 x 44.6 x 24 3 feet
T. 3-cyl. by Smith's Dock Co. Ltd., Middlesbrough.

1.1926: Completed by Smith's Dock Co. Ltd., Middlesbrough (Yard No. 820) for John Holt and Co. (Liverpool) Ltd., Liverpool as JOHN HOLT.

1937: Renamed GARTHORPE.

1939: Sold to Union of Soviet Socialist Republics, Moscow, USSR and renamed ANATOLI SEROV.

1949: Exploded a floating mine and sank in the Black Sea. (Reported March 1951).

7. JONATHAN C. HOLT/HALSTEAD 1926-1938

O.N. 147361 2,909g 1,687n 310.0 x 44.6 x 24 3 feet
T. 3-cyl. by Smith's Dock Co. Ltd., Middlesbrough.

3.1926: Completed by Smith's Dock Co. Ltd., Middlesbrough (Yard No. 821) for John Holt and Co. (Liverpool) Ltd., Liverpool as JONATHAN C. HOLT.

1937: Renamed HALSTEAD.

1938: Sold to Compania Sud Americana de Vapores, Valparaiso, Chile and renamed CACHAPOAL.

11.4.1945: Wrecked in Caleta de la Tierra, Magellan Straits whilst on a voyage from Punta Arenas with a cargo of wool and frozen meat products.

8. ROBERT L. HOLT (1) 1926-1941

O.N. 146366 2,909g 1,687n 310 0 x 44.6 x 24 3 feet
T. 3-cyl. by Smith's Dock Co. Ltd., Middlesbrough.

4.1926: Completed by Smith's Dock Co. Ltd., Middlesbrough (Yard No. 822) for John Holt and Co. (Liverpool) Ltd., Liverpool as ROBERT L. HOLT.

4.7.1941: Torpedoed and sunk by the German submarine U 69

S.S. JONATHAN. C. HOLT.

Above: Notable features of the Smith's Dock ships were the particularly long derricks on the foremast, presumably for working cargo into surf boats. This is the second of the group, JONATHAN C. HOLT.
Below: ROBERT L. HOLT (1), seen on 24th May 1935, was the only one of the 1926-trio lost during the Second World War. *[Below: F.W. Hawks]*

GODFREY B. HOLT (top) began a long association between Holts and Cammell Laird. The design has evolved, and the accommodation amidships has been trunked alongside the hatch on the bridge. GODFREY B. HOLT is leaving the South Docks at Liverpool, with the cranes of her builders' yard in the background. She was sold to Wheelock, Marden and Co. Ltd. of Hong Kong in 1951 and from 1954 until broken up in 1963 was named DORINTHIA, as which she is is seen at Cape Town on charter to Koninklijke Java-China Paketvaart Lijnen of Amsterdam (middle).

Sister to the above, THOMAS HOLT is seen below on 15th June 1934. [F.W. Hawks]

off Madeira in approximate position 24.15 north by 20.00 west whilst on a voyage from Liverpool to Freetown and Warri with general cargo. All on board were lost.

9. GODFREY B. HOLT/EUSTON 1929-1951
O.N. 161103 3,563g 2,180n 330.5 x 47.1 x 25.3 feet.
T. 3-cyl. by Cammell, Laird and Co. Ltd., Birkenhead.
21.5.1929: Launched by Cammell, Laird and Co. Ltd., Birkenhead (Yard No. 954) for John Holt and Co. (Liverpool) Ltd., Liverpool as GODFREY B. HOLT.
7.1929: Completed.
1950: Owners became John Holt Line Ltd., Liverpool.
6.1951: Renamed EUSTON.
7.1951: Sold to the Whangpoo Steamship Co. Ltd. (Wheelock, Marden and Co. Ltd., managers), Hong Kong.
1953: Renamed CARINTHIA.
1954: Renamed DORINTHIA.
8.1961: Owners became the Vega Steamship Co. Ltd. (Wheelock, Marden and Co. Ltd., managers), Hong Kong.
18.5.1963: Breaking up began by Hong Kong Rolling Mills Ltd. at Hong Kong.

10. THOMAS HOLT (2)/PADDINGTON 1929-1951
O.N. 161105 3,580g 2,191n 330.5 x 47.1 x 25.3 feet
T. 3-cyl. by Cammell, Laird and Co. Ltd., Birkenhead.
6.6.1929: Launched by Cammell, Laird and Co. Ltd., Birkenhead (Yard No. 956) for John Holt and Co. (Liverpool) Ltd., Liverpool as THOMAS HOLT.
8.1929: Completed.
1950: Owners became John Holt Line Ltd., Liverpool.
8.8.1951: Renamed PADDINGTON.
16.8.1951: Sold to F. L. Nimtz, Hamburg, Germany and renamed HANS-ERICH.
8.1952: Renamed HANS-ERICH NIMTZ.
10.1954: Sold to Mollers Ltd., London.
30.12.1954: Renamed THETA STAR.
1955: Owners became Theta Shipping Co. Ltd., Hong Kong.
25.2.1961: Aground on Etna Droogte in position 05.17.05 south by 106.54 east whilst on a voyage from Surabaya to Palembang.
26.2.1961: Refloated with extensive hull damage and taken to Djakarta.
4.5.1961: Breaking up began by the Kowloon Shipping Co. at Hong Kong.

11. JOHN HOLT (2) 1938-1941
O.N. 166235 3,815g 2,205n 390.6 x 52.8 x 20.6 feet
T. 3-cyl. and low pressure turbine by Cammell, Laird and Co. Ltd., Birkenhead.
31.3.1938: Launched by Cammell, Laird and Co. Ltd., Birkenhead (Yard No. 1030) for John Holt and Co. (Liverpool) Ltd., Liverpool as JOHN HOLT.
6.1938: Completed.

24.9.1941: Torpedoed and sunk by the German submarine U 107 north west of the Canary Islands in position 31.12 north by 23.32 west whilst on a voyage from Duala to Liverpool with 4,560 tons of produce. Of the 40 crew, 2 gunners and 9 passengers, one gunner was lost. She was sailing in convoy SL 87 at the time of her loss.

12. JONATHAN HOLT (2) 1938-1941
O.N. 166251 3,793g 2,191n 390.5 x 52.8 x 20.6 feet
T. 3-cyl. and low pressure turbine by Cammell, Laird and Co. Ltd., Birkenhead.
30.6.1938: Launched by Cammell, Laird and Co. Ltd., Birkenhead (Yard No. 1031) for John Holt and Co. (Liverpool) Ltd., Liverpool as JONATHAN HOLT.
9.1938: Completed.
24.2.1941: Torpedoed and sunk by the German submarine U 97 south west of the Faroe Islands in position 61.10 north by 11.55 west whilst on a voyage from Liverpool to West Africa with general cargo in convoy OB 289. Of the 55 crew, gunners and passengers 52 were lost.

13. JOHN HOLT (3) 1943-1944
O.N. 168853 4,964g 2,932n 390.7 x 52.8 x 29.3 feet
T. 3-cyl. and low pressure turbine by Cammell, Laird and Co. Ltd., Birkenhead.
9.12.1942: Launched by Cammell, Laird and Co. Ltd., Birkenhead (Yard No. 1112) for John Holt and Co. (Liverpool) Ltd., Liverpool as JOHN HOLT.
5.1943: Completed.
5.3.1944: Torpedoed and sunk by the German submarine U 66 off Port Harcourt in the Gulf of Guinea in position 03.56 north by 07.36 east whilst on a voyage from London and Lagos to Duala and Warri with 2,600 tons of cement and 100 tons of general cargo and mail. Of the 42 crew, 40 Kru boys and four passengers, the master and one passenger were taken prisoner on the submarine, and died when it was sunk on 6.5.1944.

14. JONATHAN HOLT (3) 1943-1962
O.N. 168865 4,963g 2,926n 390.6 x 52.8 x 29.3 feet
T. 3-cyl. and low pressure turbine by Cammell, Laird and Co. Ltd., Birkenhead.
20.7.1943: Launched by Cammell, Laird and Co. Ltd., Birkenhead (Yard No. 1113) for John Holt and Co. (Liverpool) Ltd., Liverpool as JONATHAN HOLT.
10.1943: Completed.
1950: Owners became John Holt Line Ltd., Liverpool.
11.1.1954: Owners became Guinea Gulf Line Ltd., Liverpool.
1962: Sold to the Andermatt Shipping Co., Monrovia, Liberia (Agenzia Generale Navalmarittima, Genoa, Italy) and renamed ZERMATT
18.5.1968: Arrived at Split to be broken up by Brodospas.

JOHN HOLT (2) was one of two sisters built at Birkenhead just prior to the Second World War, delightful-looking ships with raked stems and counter sterns which gave them an almost yacht-like appearance. Sadly, both sisters were torpedoed and sunk within a few months of each other in 1941. [*World Ship Photo Library*]

Above: JONATHAN HOLT (3) of 1943 was virtually a repeat of the second ship of the name. [World Ship Photo Library]

Below: The 1938 design was perpetuated in 1946, and the resulting two ships may have been unique amongst post-war newbuildings in having counter sterns. The fourth JOHN HOLT (below) survived almost until the end of Holts' independent existence. [Fotoflite incorporating Skyfotos]

ROBERT L. HOLT (2) of 1946 arriving at Swansea. *[World Ship Photo Library]*

15. **JOHN HOLT** (4) 1946-1963
O.N. 181035 3,818g 2,165n 391 x 52.8 x 20.8 feet
T. 3-cyl and low pressure turbine by Cammell, Laird and Co. Ltd., Birkenhead.
16.4.1946: Launched by Cammell, Laird and Co. Ltd., Birkenhead (Yard No. 1171) for John Holt and Co. (Liverpool) Ltd., Liverpool as JOHN HOLT.
9.1946: Completed.
1950: Owners became John Holt Line Ltd., Liverpool.
11.1.1954: Owners became Guinea Gulf Line Ltd., Liverpool.
1962: Owners became Holt Maritime Enterprises Ltd., Liverpool.
1963: Sold to Alpha Compania Naviera S.A., Panama (N. and J. Vlassopulos, London) and renamed KAVO MATAPAS under the Liberian flag.
1966: Sold to the Tung Lee Navigation Co., Monrovia, Liberia (Ta Lai Steamship Co. Ltd., Taiwan) and renamed TUNG LEE.
18.8.1968: Arrived at Kaohsiung for breaking up.

16. **ROBERT L. HOLT** (2) 1946-1962
O.N. 181040 3,819g 2,165n 391.2 x 52.8 x 20.8 feet
T. 3-cyl. and low pressure turbine by Cammell, Laird and Co. Ltd., Birkenhead.
30.7.1946: Launched by Cammell, Laird and Co. Ltd., Birkenhead (Yard No. 1172) for John Holt and Co. (Liverpool) Ltd., Liverpool as ROBERT L. HOLT.
11.1946: Completed.
1950: Owners became John Holt Line Ltd., Liverpool.
11.1.1954: Owners became Guinea Gulf Line Ltd., Liverpool.
1962: Owners became Holt Maritime Enterprises Ltd., Liverpool.
15.10.1962: Breaking up began by Jacques Bakker en Zonen, Bruges at Zelzate, Belgium.

17. **ELIZABETH HOLT** 1953-1965
O.N. 185458 5,579g 3,057n 431.8 x 60.2 x 25.6 feet
Two steam turbines double-reduction geared to a single shaft by Cammell, Laird and Co. Ltd., Birkenhead;
7.10.1952: Launched by Cammell, Laird and Co. Ltd., Birkenhead (Yard No. 1226) for John Holt Line Ltd., Liverpool as ELIZABETH HOLT.
29.1.1953: Completed.
11.1.1954: Owners became Guinea Gulf Line Ltd., Liverpool.
1963: Managers became Thos. and Jno. Brocklebank Ltd., Liverpool.

11.5.1965: Sold to the Transargo Compania Naviera S.A., Panama (Mark Scufalos, Piraeus, Greece) and renamed ADMIRALTY CREST under the Liberian flag.
1965: Renamed DESPINA N.
1971: Sold to Acamar Navigation Corporation, Monrovia, Liberia (Mark Scufalos, Piraeus, Greece).
1973: Renamed LORAIN.
21.10.1973: Arrived at Kaohsiung to be broken up by the Chuan Yuan Steel Corporation.

18. **FLORENCE HOLT** 1953-1965
O.N. 185467 5,581g 3,052n 448.8 x 60.2 x 23.2 feet
Two steam turbines double-reduction geared to a single shaft by Cammell, Laird and Co. Ltd., Birkenhead.
3.12.1952: Launched by Cammell, Laird and Co. Ltd., Birkenhead (Yard No. 1227) for John Holt Line Ltd., Liverpool as FLORENCE HOLT.
5.1953: Completed.
11.1.1954: Owners became Guinea Gulf Line Ltd., Liverpool.
1963: Managers became Thos. and Jno. Brocklebank Ltd., Liverpool.
11.5.1965: Sold to the Diana Compania Maritima S.A., Monrovia, Liberia (Mark Scufalos, Piraeus, Greece) and renamed ADMIRALTY FLYER under the Panama flag.
1965: Renamed TRIAS.
1971: Sold to Aldebaran Navigation Corporation, Monrovia, Liberia (Mark Scufalos, Piraeus, Greece).
1973: Sold to the Ardsley Shipping Corporation, Monrovia, Liberia (Mark Scufalos, Piraeus, Greece) and renamed MR. NORMAN.
1974: Renamed DAYTON
23.2.1974: Arrived at Kaohsiung to be broken up by the Nan Yung Steel and Iron Co..

19. **MARY HOLT** 1959-1965
O.N. 301319 5,577g 3,083n 463.5 x 60.0 x 24.9 fcct
Two steam turbines double-reduction geared to a single shaft by Central Marine Engine Works, West Hartlepool.
28.5.1959: Launched by William Gray and Co. Ltd., West Hartlepool (Yard No. 1300) for the Guinea Gulf Line Ltd., Liverpool as MARY HOLT.
10.1959: Completed.
1963: Managers became Thos. and Jno. Brocklebank Ltd., Liverpool.
27.9.1965: Sold to the National Shipping Corporation, Karachi, Pakistan and renamed SIPSAH.
22.11.1975: Sold to Hayden Steel Industries Ltd. to be broken up at Gadani Beach.

Above: ELIZABETH HOLT of 1953 broke away completely from the design of Holts' ships which had been developed during the early part of the century, and was a modern, composite superstructure, turbine-driven cargo liner. [Fotoflite incorporating Skyfotos]

Below: FLORENCE HOLT, sister to ELIZABETH HOLT, marked the end of a long relationship between Holts and Cammell Lairds, being the last of ten ships built and engined at Birkenhead for this small fleet. She is seen in the Canary Islands. [Jose Verwaayen]

Opposite page top: Her West Hartlepool builders gave MARY HOLT a distinctly different appearance from her Birkenhead-built predecessors. The rounded funnel top also appeared on the earlier ROSE OF LANCASTER. [Fotoflite incorporating Skyfotos]

Red Rose Navigation Co. Ltd. 1957-1965

1. ROSE OF LANCASTER 1957-1965
O.N. 187174   5,197g   2,670n   440.9 x 58.5 x 23.0 feet
Two steam turbines direct-reduction geared to a single shaft by Central Marine Engine Works, West Hartlepool;
29.7.1957: Launched by William Gray and Co. Ltd., West Hartlepool (Yard No. 1290) for the Red Rose Navigation Co. Ltd., Hamilton, Bermuda as ROSE OF LANCASTER.
12.1957: Completed.
11.5.1965: Sold to Splosna Plovidba, Piran, Yugoslavia and renamed BOCNA.
23.3.1978: Arrived at Split to be broken up by Brodospas.

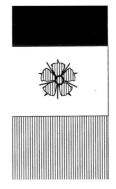
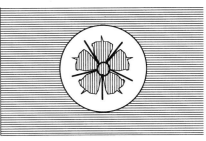

Flag and funnel of Red Rose Navigation Co. Ltd. 1957-1965 *[J.L. Loughran]*

Red Rose Navigation Co. Ltd. of Bermuda owned the delightfully-named ROSE OF LANCASTER which was operated as a unit of Holts' fleet. She is seen in her owners' distinctive funnel colours, but she later ran with Guinea Gulf's funnel.
[Author's collection]

BAZELEYS OF PENZANCE AND THE LITTLE WESTERN STEAMSHIP COMPANY
Part one
Tony Pawlyn

In the late 1870s a small Penzance firm of millers and provision merchants established a modest line of coastal steamships which became highly respected. Trading under the title Little Western Steamship Company, George Bazeley and his sons ran a service between London and Bristol for forty years. During this period they earned a reputation for punctuality and regularity that was second-to-none in a highly competitive trade. Handling increasing quantities of cargo and passengers, by 1912 they were putting 63,000 tons of freight through Bristol City Docks. Still in good shape at the end of the First World War, the firm was bought by Coast Lines Ltd. in 1920.

George Bazeley and Sons

In 1864 George Bazeley came to Penzance and joined the established firm of Samuel Higgs and Son. Higgs had built up a strong local trade as general, grocery and provision merchants, and as corn factors and millers. When Higgs died in April 1874, George succeeded to the business and then began trading as George Bazeley and Sons of the Albert Stores, Penzance. In time his sons - George Paulle, William James, and Sidney Godolphin Bazeley - joined him. A progressive firm, they introduced steam machinery into their milling business at Gulval (just east of Penzance) along with mechanical ice production - then a great novelty and boon to the fishing industry. Their business prospered and during the late 1870s and early 1880s Bazeleys were consignees of regular grain imports into Penzance, carried in foreign-going sailing vessels of 600 to 800 tons. With their steam-mills in full production, Bazeleys were producing flour and meal in excess of local consumption. They already relied on the local mineral schooners for their supplies of steam-coal, but now needed an economic means of access to markets for their surplus flour. It was at this juncture that George Bazeley bought his first vessel, the 105-ton schooner BETA, in 1875.

The BETA was a relatively new vessel, having been built at Portsmouth in 1873 for the Mediterranean and North African trade, and was so employed under the command of Captain William Meads. Her registry was transferred from Portsmouth to Penzance on 16th April 1875 with George Bazeley as her sole owner. However, it is quite possible that he employed her prior to this date.

Manned by a crew of six, BETA was commanded by Thomas Beckerleg. Although essentially employed in the home trade, she did make the occasional foreign trade voyage under Bazeleys' ownership. One such was from Briton Ferry to Marans (probably Marrenes on the coast of France just south of La Rochelle) in 1875-76. For this voyage, Captain Beckerleg, who did not at that time have a certificate of competency, went as 'Bosun' at £5 per month, and one John James was shipped as master for that voyage only. For the remainder of 1876 she made two direct voyages to and from Penzance and South Wales ports, and five round voyages between Penzance, South Wales ports, and Chatham, Sheerness, or London. On the Thames she berthed alongside the old South Devon Wharf, on the eastern side of the entrance to St. Catherine's Dock, and there loaded general cargoes for Penzance.

While no cargo details have survived for these voyages, contacts were made, and ideas were conceived that later resulted in the formation of Bazeleys' coastal steamship line. Warehouses were established at Cardiff and Swansea to receive surplus flour from Penzance, so flour was clearly a key element of their trade. Coal no doubt formed another, but there is no positive evidence as to what else was coming down from London to Penzance. It was probably groceries and manufactured goods, and in this emulated the now-defunct Penzance Shipping Company. They had run small smacks and schooners between London and Penzance from 1815 to 1873 when they were forced out of business by steam competition from the London-Liverpool line of steamers managed by Samuel Hough.

The 'Alpha Line of Traders'

In 1877 Gorge Bazeley acquired a second schooner, the older LADY RODNEY. She had been built at Salcombe in 1865 and, like the BETA before her, had spent some time in the Mediterranean and North African trade. Although smaller than the BETA at 90 tons, in Bazeleys' advertisements she was described as of 165 tons burden. Later records confirm that she consistently carried 165 tons of coal and macadam (crushed roadstone) in the summer months.

Somewhat perversely for a second vessel, Bazeley renamed her ALPHA, but this was possibly because in her he really saw the vision of a regular line of vessels. Under the command of Captain Richard Boase Kelynack, she was employed mainly in the Penzance-Bristol service. Bazeleys came to call this service their 'Alpha Line of Traders,' though they only ever employed the one vessel. Like the BETA, the ALPHA also made occasional foreign trade voyages. One was from Penzance to Palermo, Gallipoli, and back to Goole, between October 1877 and April 1878. Not then holding a 'ticket', Kelynack did not go on this voyage but resumed his command at Plymouth on 20th May. For the rest of 1878 the ALPHA was employed between Penzance and Bristol, making ten round voyages, with two intermediate calls at Cardiff on the way down from Bristol.

The first steamer

Meanwhile, Bazeleys' had planned their next move. Perhaps they were spurred on by the failure of the late Penzance Shipping Company to adopt steam propulsion, and their ultimate demise in 1873. They had also witnessed the success of Samuel Hough's steamers in the London-Liverpool trade, which had commenced calling at Penzance each way in 1868. Bazeleys now decided to venture into small steamers and in September 1877 George Bazeley negotiated the purchase of the French iron screw steamer PROGRES. Just five years old, she was a modest 210 tons gross and was put under the command of Captain William Beckerleg, a brother to Tom of the BETA. Bazeleys now set out to establish themselves in the Penzance-London trade:

'Penzance October 2nd 1877 - The screw steamer PROGRES, by means of which Messrs. Bazeley & Sons hope to develop a regular trade between Penzance, London

The schooner to the right in this classic view of Mount's Bay is believed to be George Bazeley's ALPHA. *[F. Gibson]*

and South Wales, arrived in this harbour this morning, on its first trip from London. The venture looks promising, for more goods were offered to the steamer at the South Devon Wharf, London, than she could carry.'

Her first set of British home trade half-year crew agreements commenced before she was technically a British vessel. Not registered at Penzance until 30th October 1878, her crew agreement opened on 8th October with the signing on of her crew at Penzance. By this date she had already made one round voyage between Penzance and Cardiff, presumably under the French flag - possibly as a trial trip to ensure that she was suitable for the trade. She completed another round voyage between Penzance, Cardiff, Sheerness, London and Penzance before she was formally registered at Penzance as the sole property of George Bazeley. She was either not well suited to Cardiff or Cardiff to her, or the trading conditions there proved disadvantageous. On her third trip to South Wales her port of call was changed to Swansea, and this now became Bazeleys' Welsh terminal.

With an advertised burthen of 350 tons, PROGRES had over double the cargo carrying capacity of either of the two schooners. Even so, it was insufficient for the initial flurry of trade as on her first two departures from London cargo had to be left behind. From the advertisements it would appear that this was partially caused by the late delivery of goods to the South Devon Wharf for onward shipment.

'Goods intended for this boat should be at the Wharf, London, at least one day previous to the date of sailing. Delivery within the Borough of Penzance undertaken if desired, at one penny per hundredweight on quantities over two hundredweights. Insurance affected at 3s.4d. per cent during the winter months.'

Freight rates were not advertised but agents were soon appointed at her regular ports of call. W. Gage Jacobs was appointed as the Company's London agent, and initially their London depot was established at the South Devon

Wharf. At Swansea, J. W. Pockett, of COLLIER (205/1848) renown, with offices at the entrance to South Dock, was appointed as their agent. Soon after entering service, the PROGRES was advertised to call at Padstow where J. England was appointed as local agent. Although by July 1878 their advertisements were headed *'Steam Communication between London and Penzance; Penzance and Swansea; and London, Padstow, and Wadebridge'*, the PROGRES may only have 'called off', as Padstow does not appear in the ports of call listed in her early crew agreements.

Nominally providing a round service from Penzance to Swansea via Padstow to London, and back to Penzance, arrangements were flexible during those early years. As opportunities presented, the steamer was diverted, and George Bazeley also seems to have maintained contact with her former owners in France. On many occasions during 1877 and 1878, she called into French channel ports on her way up to the Thames, making seven calls at Caen, four at Rouen, three at Havre, two each at Trouville and Dieppe; and once at Fecamp during 1878. The nature of any cargo embarked at these ports is not known, but may have been vegetables. Equally, PROGRES may only have been delivering coal from South Wales.

The intention seems to have been to establish a fortnightly schedule, but in practice the service took between 16 and 20 days per round voyage, especially with calls on the French coast. The pressures on maintaining even this schedule with a single steamship were considerable. In trying to establish a reputation for punctuality and reliability a punishing schedule had to be kept, and Bazeleys were quick to publicise any fast passages.

'November 6th 1877 - arrived in London on Saturday morning 45 hours from Penzance.' And: 'December 25th, 1877 - had a splendid run of 36 hours to the Downs, but was detained 24 hours in the river by a dense fog.'

Accidents and repairs

Even with the best of management and skilful ship handling risks were taken and short cuts made to keep up the service schedule, and accidents were inevitable. There is no suggestion that either Bazeleys or their masters were any better or worse than the norm - though their reputation would suggest the former - but accidents there were. The first occurred on 11th December when, in leaving London, the PROGRES was fouled by the ECHO (240/1868). Although no serious damage had been sustained, and the cargo was undamaged, it was sufficient to detain the PROGRES in the Thames for two or three days. Occurring on her homeward leg, this detention resulted in a nine-day passage to Penzance.

Like many early steamers, PROGRES was somewhat underpowered, and soon after her acquisition extensive work was required to bring her up to par. In February 1878 she was sent round to Harvey and Co. Ltd. at Hayle, for a refit that took nearly four weeks which included:

a new engine-room floor, ladder and companion
re-turning the screw shaft and re-boring the stern tube
turning pistons and rings, feed poles and cross-heads
planing, surfacing and refitting cylinders, slide valves, link and slot-link gear
repairing the steam whistle and gauge cocks
repairing and refitting her donkey engine
providing new stays for the telegraph.

In addition, her cylinders were given new yellow-pine casings, with lashings of tar and paint, graining and varnish being applied to the whole vessel. In all, her refit cost £296 5s. 1d., which seems a modest enough sum today, but was not considered cheap at the time. Following this refit she still lacked steam-generating capacity, and in June she was again in the hands of Harveys. This time alterations were made to her boilers, which included fitting ten Galloway's tubes, and substantial repairs to the boiler shell. This work probably increased her boiler pressure as well as the volume of steam generated, and it seems to have done the job when normal service was resumed.

Constantly working round the Land's End, and in the mouths of the English and Bristol Channels, the PROGRES inevitably met heavy weather. In November 1878, while on passage from Swansea to Trouville and the Thames, even before she cleared the Bristol Channel she was punching into the teeth of a south-westerly snorter. Such heavy seas were encountered off St. Ives that the engineers and stokers had to be battened down below to prevent serious flooding of the engine-room - thank goodness for the new engine-room companion. As it was she was eight days making that passage - the longest for the year - having achieved an average of two days at sea and two days in ports throughout 1878. In all, allowing for the four weeks under refit, she completed 19 round voyages between London and the south-west.

Ever keen to stress the speedy nature of their service, Bazeleys did not always release the full story to the press. One report published in January 1878, exudes speed and power, stating that:

'The s.s. PROGRES arrived at Penzance, at five a.m. on Saturday, steaming straight up to her wharf, and commenced discharging soon after. She was 42 hours from the Thames, having had strong weather and snowstorms most of the way.'

Details of this voyage show that she was, in fact, four days coming down from London, so she must have been detained in the Thames for two days, but this was not mentioned.

The ALPHA continued to meet the needs of the Bristol-Penzance service. In addition to modest amounts of flour (little more than ballast at times) there were regular shipments of macadam from Penlee quarry - through the little fishing harbour at Mousehole prior to the completion of the new South Pier at Newlyn in 1886. Although paying minimal freight, the regular shipments of macadam for Bristol helped underpin the financial viability of this service. BETA continued to run in the Penzance-Cardiff trade, taking up flour and bringing back steam coal. It was on one of these voyages that she had her first collision. In February 1879 an iron steamer ran into her but came off worst. Having left Cardiff with coal for Penzance and being becalmed some five miles north east of Hurleston Point, Captain Beckerleg brought the BETA up to an anchor. At about 8.00 pm the lookout reported an approaching steamer's masthead and port light on the port bow. After much shouting by her crew and putting their helm hard a'starboard to try and veer off in the stream, the steamer came on to run into them at full speed. At just the last moment the steamer began to turn, and her bow just cleared the BETA's headgear. But, as she drove past, her stern slewed across and the BETA's bowsprit went right through the engine room. The steamer was cut down to well below the waterline and quickly filled and sank just after the crew had taken to their boat. Although the BETA was in a sad state with all her headgear carried away, and her foremast threatening to fall at any moment, she was not making any water. Unable to set any headsails, Beckerleg eventually got her back to Cardiff, where she spent six weeks under repair. The steamer proved to be the French FALCONIER, and her master's story was that he mistook the BETA's light for that of a pilot-cutter, and when he finally took avoiding action, with the wheel hard over, one of the steering chains broke, and she swept onto the schooner.

Crew problems

One peculiarity of the West Cornwall mineral schooners was the payment of voyage money in addition to the normal wages. At this time voyage money stood at 10 shillings per round voyage between Penzance, St. Ives, Hayle or Portreath and the Welsh ports. With these schooners making from fifteen to twenty round voyages a year, the additional £7.10s to £10 was a very significant addition to an AB's wages of £2 15s. to £3 5s. a month.

In April 1879, with freight rates low, the Penzance owners decided to put a stop to voyage money, and the local mariners went on strike. The ALPHA's crew were amongst them. Having just loaded 160 tons of macadam at Mousehole, she was nearly be-neaped by the backing tides. But, assisted by two other schooner masters, Captain Kelynack was just able to get her over to Penzance before she became stuck at Mousehole for a fortnight or so. The BETA's crew were also on strike:

'The colliers' crews still hold out against the 'docking' of the 10s. voyage-money, and their offer to accept 5s. has been refused by the owners, who say that the Hayle crews get no voyage-money, and that the men at Cardiff and Neath are glad of berths at £2 15s. and £2 10s. a month less than the Penzance men get without reckoning voyage-money. Crews for the ALPHA and BETA were engaged at Plymouth, but they refused to come when they heard there was a strike. The ALPHA, however got away on Sunday, but had to return to the Bay. She was off again on Monday just after the BETA sailed.'

It was always thus with the rivalry between 'company' ships. No matter what the conditions, once one master made a break for sea, any others had to follow!

There was no indication in the newspaper report as to who was crewing the ALPHA and BETA on this occasion. Nor yet whether the strike had been settled. And the wages implied in the report do not compute, as working for '£2 15s. to £2 10s. a month less than the Penzance men' would have equalled working for nothing! So the suggestion that Neath and Cardiff hands were prepared to work for nearly half-wages was a gross piece of deception. Throughout Bazeleys' time as owners, all hands on their vessels had to find their own food. This meant that they were paid a little above the going monthly rates, but not to the extent of the full 1/6d. per day allowed for 'sufficient without waste!'

Some months later, although both schooners were back in service, tensions were still running high when Bazeleys brought charges of desertion against two seamen off the ALPHA. During the trial report it emerged that only one of them had, in fact, signed articles. After having been paid off at the end of the last voyage, seaman Albert Whittington of Lydney agreed to sign on for another term at £3 5s. a month. Having joined ship on the Saturday morning, and after having worked cargo for some hours, Whittington and the other hands all walked ashore, having 'agreed not to sail any longer at the reduced scale of wages.' Two of the hands relented and eventually returned to work, but Whittington and Nicholls did not. Whittington had signed articles on 1st July, and had not since given any notice, so was clearly in breach of the law. On realising this in court, he offered to return and work out his notice to the next port; however, Bazeleys would have none of this, and had instructed Captain Beckerleg not to take him back. While the case against Nicholls fell, as he had not signed articles, that against Whittington stood and, however reluctantly, the magistrates were obliged to order his imprisonment for four weeks.

The Little Western Steamship Company.

PROGRES had established a firm hold on the Penzance-London-Swansea trade and, whenever her schedule coincided with those of the ALPHA or the BETA, she would give them a helping tow for part of the way. Such gratuitous assistance helped the 'Alpha Line' keep up a frequent if slightly irregular service, but was no substitute for a full steam schedule. By early 1880 Bazeleys were resolved to put a steamer on their Bristol service, but first they had to find a suitable vessel. As it happened, a virtually new steamship now came on the market, but one which had already had an ignominious, if brief, career. She was the 317-ton WILLIAM J. TAYLOR of Newcastle-upon-Tyne.

Built in 1879, she had a disastrous and incomplete maiden voyage. Named WILLIAM J. TAYLOR after her first owner, she left the Tyne for London, only to suffer a major failure of one of her cylinders. Limping back to the Tyne, she was struck by a German ship, almost cut in two, and foundered within the port limits. Shortly afterwards the wreck was successfully raised, docked and the damage made good. Now placed on the market, she was acquired by Bazeleys. The terms and conditions under which she was acquired are not known, but she was in their employ for quite some time before her registration was transferred to Penzance. Making her first voyage from London to Penzance between 26th and 29th June 1880, she was not registered at Penzance until 21st April 1881.

With the arrival of the WILLIAM J. TAYLOR, Bazeleys launched their Little Western Steamship Company, while winding up their Alpha Line of Traders. Running in conjunction with the PROGRES, the new concern intended one of their vessels to leave London and Bristol every Saturday, with intermediate calls at Torquay and Penzance. Allowing four days for the passage between London and Bristol, the new service commenced on Saturday 26th June 1880. Even with two steamers, this was a tough schedule to keep up week in and week out.

After only a few months under Bazeleys' flag the WILLIAM J. TAYLOR had a near miss with the viaduct carrying the new harbour road at Penzance. Forced back to Penzance by a November storm, she drove in through the harbour mouth at some speed and with engines going full astern her weigh was checked just in time as she careered across the harbour. Just missing the new swing-bridge at the end of the viaduct, she caught her forefoot on the adjacent slipway, but no major damage was done.

During this same period the PROGRES was also involved in several incidents. On 8th October 1880 she arrived at Penzance from Bristol towing a ship's lifeboat. On board were seven hands taken up from the boat, after having previously abandoned the Newhaven brig HENRY BENNESS (168/1839). Bound for Newcastle from Gloucester with 272 tons of salt, the brig had encountered heavy head seas off the Lizard the previous day. Plunging into one particularly large sea, she was brought up all standing, and carried away her jib-boom, bulwarks and topgallant mast and started her bow planking. Making water fast, the salt cargo was washed into the pumps, which soon became choked. About 2.00 am, when off the Longships and with her decks almost flush with the sea, the crew were forced to abandon ship. The PROGRES came up with them a little after 6.00 am, near the Brissons, picking up the crew and taking their boat in tow.

Only a month later PROGRES was in collision with the ketch JAMES WALTER (75/1863) off Lundy. She inflicted extensive damage on the ketch, carrying away her bowsprit, knight's head, cut-water and stem. But the ketch remained afloat, and the PROGRES later arrived at Bristol with considerable damage to her starboard bow.

The WILLIAM J. TAYLOR's career with Bazeleys was short. On the evening of 28th September 1881 she was heading into the mouth of the Thames about 9.00 pm, via the Warp Channel. It was dark but clear. Three or four miles above the Mouse Light she came up on a barque anchored in the fairway. Passing some 200 yards to the south of the barque, those on the bridge picked up the lights of a steamer coming down. Captain Kelynack ordered 'Hard a port!' but a few minutes later she was struck on the port side just forward of the bridge. The two steamers collided with considerable force and the other's stem cut deep into the WILLIAM J. TAYLOR as far as her hatch combings. The other steamer proved to be the General Steam Navigation Company's PLOVER (947/1875), bound from London to Hamburg. At 231 feet she was considerably larger than the WILLIAM J. TAYLOR and, locked into her side for a time, the PLOVER's bow reared many feet above her deck. A breach six or seven feet wide from deck to bilge was opened and the water began to flood in. Although the PLOVER's bow was also damaged, this damage was above the water line about the level of the TAYLOR's deck. The PLOVER's master at once took in the gravity of the situation, and kept his engines working ahead to try and plug the breach while the crew abandoned ship. In the space of a few minutes all had scrambled, or been hauled, on board the PLOVER - eleven crew plus two passengers and a baby.

The watch below had to abandon ship in various states of undress and none of the crew escaped with more than they stood up in. Fortunately, only one man was injured - Henry Lander, one of the firemen, cut his bare feet badly on the jagged deck as he swung himself up onto the WILLIAM J. TAYLOR's bridge, the better to climb aboard the PLOVER.

In the rush to abandon ship her engines had been left at half-ahead and the two steamers now worked apart with the sinking vessel steaming round in a circle. Now that some calm had descended on the scene there seemed a chance of running her ashore, and so the PLOVER's boat was sent away under her mate, and manned by Captain Kelynack, his brother - mate of the WILLIAM J. TAYLOR - and Albert Merrifield, her engineer. On reaching her they found her foredeck under water, but the chief engineer boarded her and to the alarm of all went below decks to save two suits of clothes! Moments later the chief was again taken off but nothing could be done to save the steamer. About 30 minutes after the collision the WILLIAM J. TAYLOR plunged to the bottom in eight or nine fathoms of water.

Although there was no loss of life the WILLIAM J. TAYLOR was carrying 100 tons of palm oil; 150 tons of galvanised iron products; as well as other items, valued at a total of £8,000. In contrast, the PLOVER was carrying £50,000 of bullion. At the Board of Trade enquiry both masters were found equally responsible and each side had to bear their own costs. Fortunately for Bazeleys they were fully insured for both the vessel and her cargo. And there matters may well have remained. For many years the wreck of the WILLIAM J. TAYLOR was no serious threat to navigation, although she was 'blown down' by explosives at some time. About 1968, the Port of London Authority wished to establish a 50 feet deep clear anchorage for a new generation of large tankers near the Black Tail Spit Buoy. Just to the south west of the buoy their surveyors had detected a bank with only 39 feet of water over it. On investigation this proved to be a wreck site banked up with silt, and had to be removed. During the early stages of its removal the wreck was positively identified as the WILLIAM J. TAYLOR when a grab brought up her main beam, duly marked with her Official Number 80557. Most of what was recovered was just a heap of mangled metal, and a quantity of stinking bullocks' horns and hooves. But, amongst all this scrap was discovered a beautiful cast-brass cabin stair tread featuring Neptune supported by two fanciful dolphins. And, despite the evil-smelling mixture of clay, silt, horns and hooves, when broken pieces of her hold ceiling were brought up there was a strong smell of pine.

On learning of the loss of the WILLIAM J. TAYLOR Bazeleys immediately made arrangements to hire a relief steamer. It is not known why she was available at such short notice, but within days the STOCKTON had been chartered and cleared out of London on her first passage to Penzance and Bristol. Owned by the Stockton and London Screw Steamship Co., the STOCKTON was relatively old, having been completed in 1856, but was one of the fastest steamers on the London run, normally making the return voyage in less than a week. In 1881 the rival Tees Union Shipping Company was formed, and with the STOCKTON now 25 years old it was probably an opportune moment for the Stockton and London company to dispose of her.

Just prior to her leaving the Stockton-London service, the STOCKTON was rigged as a three-masted schooner with an elegant, if by then dated, clipper bow. She carried a midships bridge fore side of the mainmast (the main shrouds being attached to the bridge wing housing), with engines aft and a slightly raised quarterdeck. A small deck saloon-cum-cabin was located on the upper deck just forward of the bridge. On the starboard side aft, just forward of the engineroom casing, stood a vertical donkey boiler with its chimney carried into her funnel by a cranked offset flue.

For three months STOCKTON filled in as a hired vessel, commanded by one Hitcher or Hitchens. She was quickly in the news: one Monday morning, as she was leaving Penzance for Bristol, her chief engineer mistook 'full astern' for 'full ahead' and she drove into the Amsterdam schooner FENNA WILLEMINA (129 tons) with great force. The schooner was loaded with timber from Maracaibo and this no doubt helped keep her afloat while she was warped up to the Albert Wharf. Meanwhile the STOCKTON being unhurt, *'The accident did not delay the steamer, which taking a rope from the schooner ALPHA, off the Extension, towed her round land.'*

Having proved herself on charter, STOCKTON was bought by Bazeleys and registered at Penzance under George Bazeleys' ownership on 24th January 1882. At about the same time Bazeleys acquired another more modern steamer, the ACACIA. She made her first appearance at Penzance on 4th December 1881, on route from Bristol to London. Command of the ACACIA was given to R. B. Kelynack, late of the ill-fated WILLIAM J. TAYLOR, while command of the STOCKTON was given to one George Parry. In all probability the ACACIA was acquired first, but this double purchase stretched the family concern's finances to the limit. When registered at Penzance, the STOCKTON was under mortgage to one John Milner Lennard for £2,625 at 10% interest. But business was good and the mortgage was discharged after twelve months.

The chief attraction of both the ACACIA and the STOCKTON was their relative power and speed. Both had engines of 80 BHP and, the STOCKTON having proved that she could maintain the fortnightly London-Bristol schedule, the ACACIA was expected to match this. While she steamed quite well she was rather cranky, a trait which caused some problems with close manoeuvring, as we shall see later. ACACIA was a transitional design three-island type steamer, with engines aft. Her bridge was formed by the midships island, with a light flying bridge above on stanchions over a small chart-house. The two lifeboats were chocked-up on transverse skids off the fore side of the bridge. Between the boats an upright donkey boiler was mounted on the upper deck between the bridge and the fore hold. In all her superstructure was a very exposed and flimsy piece of construction.

STOCKTON at Stockton about 1882 before she was acquired by Bazeleys. Note the cranes on deck and the donkey boiler aft with the offset flue carried into the funnel. *[Peter Barton collection]*

ACACIA at Bristol about 1883 under Harrison's ownership. *[Bristol City Museum, York collection, P.3743M]*

A potentially dangerous fire was extinguished just in time on one of the ACACIA's first calls at Penzance. Having discharged her cargo, some spilt oil - which had soaked into the pine ceiling of the hold - caught fire. While the initial blast of flame leapt above bridge height, no blast damage occurred to the vessel. With great presence of mind the stevedores and crew tipped macadam into the hold and smothered the fire.

With the two new steamers on the London-Bristol service, the PROGRES was at first put on the Penzance-South Wales service, carrying coal down and flour and other cargo up. But during February 1882 she was laid up, possibly under repair, but there is some indication that she was being kept in strategic reserve in case of need on the London-Bristol service. But, with the main service running without any major hitches, Bazeley now tried to branch out by breaking into the Penzance-Liverpool trade. This new service was first advertised on 23rd February 1882:

'STEAM FROM PENZANCE TO LIVERPOOL - The Little Western Steamship Company intend running their steamer PROGRES between Penzance and Liverpool every ten days, calling at intermediate ports if sufficient inducement is offered.'

Captain Kelynack was now given command of the PROGRES to pioneer this new service, while command of the ACACIA was given to Captain R. A. Spray of Hayle, after a Captain Bevan moved on after only one month in Bazeleys' employ. Between March and mid-May she made a number of Liverpool voyages, with calls at Swansea to take up Welsh steam coal. But the service was not well patronised, and by mid May she had to be withdrawn to bolster the London-Bristol service. With Captain Spray having just assumed command, towards the end of March the ACACIA was involved in an incident that highlighted her crankiness. As the *Cornish Telegraph* of 29th March reported:

'COLLISION AT SEA. - A Good Friday incident at Penzance that created considerable interest was the return to harbour of the Little Western Steamship Co.'s steamer ACACIA, Captain Spray, and the same owners' schooner ALPHA, Captain T. Beckerleg. On the Wednesday previous the steamer left for Bristol, having in tow the schooner (in ballast) bound to Porthcawl. At night the wind freshened from the N.E., with a heavy sea, and when off St. Ive's Bay,

Godrevey light bearing S.E., eight miles distant, the ropes parted. About midnight the ACACIA ran alongside the schooner at half-speed, to get a line on board. Just then a heavy sea struck the ALPHA, and swung her round onto the steamer. The schooner's bows crushed in the stern of the lifeboat, and then sweeping aft, carried away the flying bridge and telegraph, the main rigging, the funnel of the donkey steamer, the mizen mast and the whole of the starboard rails, besides smashing in the companion of the cabin by means of the boat's davits. The top of the mainmast was also broken off, and the main funnel narrowly escaped. The schooner lost her bowsprit and head gear, and had her cutwater smashed, besides doing damage to her bows. The steamer kept the schooner company all night, and at daybreak, at considerable risk, took her again in tow. All Thursday they sheltered in Whitesand Bay, and cleared away the wreckage, and on Friday returned to Penzance. Captain Spray had a narrow escape. At the time of the collision he was on the flying bridge and fell to the bridge below, but fortunately was not hurt.'

No blame was attributed to Captain Spray, who went on to become one of Bazeleys' senior captains, but both the ACACIA and the ALPHA had to be pulled out of service for several weeks for the necessary repairs. No sooner had the ACACIA returned to service at the end of May, than the STOCKTON had to be taken out of service during June and July. About this time Captain Parry left Bazeleys' employ, and command of the STOCKTON passed to Captain Jacob Hodge. Hodge was later to become Bazeleys' senior captain, commanding each new acquisition in turn over the next twenty-five years. The cause of STOCKTON's withdrawal at this time has not been discovered, but it was to cover this interruption that the PROGRES was returned to the London-Bristol service.

In one respect the older STOCKTON was clearly superior to the newer ACACIA. While both had donkey boilers to provide auxiliary steam for deck winches and windlass, the STOCKTON had deck cranes serving both holds, rather than relying on swinging gaffs. This facility greatly speeded up cargo handling when there were no available dockside cranes, and was one that was carried into most of Bazeleys later steamers. In many ways Bazeleys were still searching for the right kind of steamer for their service.

During the second half of 1882 the PROGRES continued to provide a mixed service. Demand on the Liverpool route never came up to expectations, this port being very well served by a number of other coastal liner services. Sailings settled at roughly one a month, with PROGRES completing seven such voyages, which were punctuated by five Swansea-Caen voyages, and a couple of London voyages at the end of the year. ACACIA and STOCKTON provided the bulk of the London-Bristol service and the company's reputation began to grow.

One aspect of such a service schedule was the increasing demand for bunker coal. By the 1880s the efficiency of marine steam engines had improved to a very economic level. But, while the triple-expansion engines allowed even longer voyages at reduced coal consumption per rated power, their much higher cost compared with compound engines acted as a barrier to their general adoption by coastal steamers - at least up until the 1890s. Coal was relatively cheap and usually available in most British ports, so as long as coastal steamers could run for a week or so without bunkering, this was sufficient for the general needs of these craft. Bazeleys' steamers probably carried coal for a fortnight, as they bunkered at Bristol, with small stocks being held at the ports of call for emergencies. As a small company with a relatively modest bulk demand for steam coal, Bazeleys may have been paying a premium for their coal at Bristol. Whatever, in May 1883 they acquired an old Admiralty ketch, the QUEEN, and established her as their collier at Bristol. Of unknown age she was a heavily-built product of HM Dockyards. Crewed by her master and two ABs she would pop over to Cardiff or Newport and load steam coal back to Bristol. There she would lie as a floating depot to bunker Bazeleys' steamers before making another short trip to replenish her stocks.

Although a modern steamer, there was something not quite right about ACACIA, and she changed hands quite frequently. Completed in 1879 for James S. Campbell of Dublin, she was sold to George Kerr of Glasgow in 1880, and Bazeleys acquired her late in 1881. In November 1883 Bazeleys were to sell her on to John Harrison. Replaced by the THAMES, the ACACIA remained registered at Penzance until the mortgage was cleared in June 1886, when she was transferred to London.

Their choice of the THAMES reflected Bazeleys' satisfaction with the STOCKTON. A younger product of Pearse and Co.'s Stockton yard in 1866, she too was built for the Stockton and London Screw Steamship Co. Apart from a straight stem she was of a very similar appearance and size, and had an identical set of 80 BHP compound engines. The THAMES was not registered at Penzance until 8th May 1886, but was clearly in Bazeleys' employ from September 1883, if not a little earlier.

Captain Hodge was given initial command of the THAMES, which was first reported leaving Penzance for London on 5th September 1883. Captain Spray then moved over to the STOCKTON from the ACACIA, while Captain Kelynack delivered the latter vessel to her new owners in London before resuming command of the PROGRES.

Over the years Bazeleys' shoreside arrangements also underwent a number of changes. On the Thames the berth at the South Devon Wharf proved unsuitable for the larger steamers now being employed, and had no spare capacity for increased business. In January 1884 Bazeleys' shifted their London terminal to the Free Trade Wharf, Broad Street - about a mile and a half further down the Thames - where the wharves had a much easier road access and were situated close to the mouth of the Rotherhithe Tunnel. This berth remained Bazeleys' London terminal for the next 36 years.

The year 1884 also saw the completion on the long awaited floating dock basin at Penzance, and with this and superior wharfage on the Thames, Bazeleys now set about enhancing their London-Bristol service.

[To be continued]

A view of Penzance Harbour about 1890, showing the newly-completed floating dock, with the hulk of the LUCIEN alongside the north wall. A sister to Bazeley's ALBERT, she was owned by the Penzance Dry Dock, Coal and Trading Company who used her as a coal barge, towing her to and from South Wales ports. The end of Bazeleys' sheds are just showing on the extreme left, with the Trinity House depot behind. *[National Maritime Museum, Francis Frith 40603]*

PUTTING BLUE FUNNEL STRAIGHT

We were not surprised that *Ships in Focus Blue Funnel Line* has generated much interest and correspondence since it was published in November 1998, but we were particularly gratified that correspondents could find relatively few errors. Below we collate the corrections, comments and additions; and include some more detail of one of Blue Funnel's best-photographed casualties, the grounding of the PATROCLUS near Portland in 1907.

Casualty corrections

The most embarassing errors arose through the authors' ignorance of naval affairs during the Second World War. Firstly, the EURYLOCHUS (page 59) was not in convoy at the time she was sunk by the raider KORMORAN. As Derek Atherton points out, German auxiliary cruisers did not attack convoys, and EURYLOCHUS had left the convoy when it dispersed on 19th January 1941. Secondly, MENELAUS (page 73) was not in the Mediterranean when sunk by ADMIRAL HIPPER, although she was in a convoy. She was actually some 700 nautical miles west of Cape Finisterre when convoy WS5A was attacked by the German heavy cruiser at first light on Christmas Day 1940. The escorting cruisers HMS BERWICK and HMS BONAVENTURE engaged the ADMIRAL HIPPER, which escaped in the prevailing low visibility. Thirdly, the survivors from the AENEAS (page 49) could not have been picked up by a HMS WORTHINGTON: no such ship existed. As well as Derek, we thank Bob Todd for advice on these points.

Our biggest embarassment was reserved for the caption beneath the photograph of EURYMEDON on page 79. A late change to the typesetting - after it had been checked five times - meant that the last lines of this caption fell off. The last sentence should have read: 'However, nothing could be done to save the vessel and just prior to her sinking on 27th September the remaining personnel were taken off by HMCS OTTAWA.' Two errors in spellings of ship's names have been pointed out to us by Christy MacHale. The EMPIRE HAMBLE (page 105) became the Thai THEPSATRI NAWA, whilst the MACHAON became Glen Line's GLENAFFARIC in 1935. Even Holts seem to have difficulty with the spelling of the latter name: they used GLENAFFRIC when they renamed the NESTOR (4) in 1968, as we correctly reported on page 146. Keith Lewis tells us that the fire on the PYRRHUS in November 1964 took place whilst she was in West Huskisson Dock, Liverpool.

Casualty confirmations

In some cases we quoted alternative identities for the submarines which sank Blue Funnel ships, or were unable to identify the boats concerned. Again, Derek and Bob have provided confirmation of these.

The submarine which attacked ASCANIUS (page 49) in the English Channel on 30th July 1944 was U 621. AGAPENOR (page 52) was sunk by U 87; it could not have been U 57 which was based at Gotenhafen in the Baltic as a training boat from 1941 to 1945. Sinking of LAERTES (page 63) off Florida on 3rd May 1942 is credited to U 109. Of the other possibilities cited, U 564 is credited with sinking the OCEAN VENUS (7,174/1941) in the same position earlier that day, whilst U 98 had no success in the area on this patrol. The Japanese submarine which attacked ASPHALION (page 78) in the Bay of Bengal was identified as the Japanese Ro-110, and in fact was sunk by the escort of convoy JC36, the Royal Indian Navy sloop JUMNA, HMAS IPSWICH and HMAS LAUNCESTON. The SEBASTIANO VENIER, formerly JASON (page 98), was damaged by HMS PORPOISE on 9th December 1941 but was actually sunk by HMS TORBAY off Cape Methene on 15th December 1941. There were over two thousand prisoners-of-war on board, but the hospital ship ARNO (8,024/1912) was able to rescue some 1,800.

Pilgrim trade origins

Peter Newall's article on pilgrim ships in *Record* 9 prompted Richard Cornish to point out that the original 'deck passengers' carried by the Blue Funnel 'pilgrim' ships were Chinese workers travelling from Amoy down to the Straits and Singapore. The pilgrim service began after this. Initially pilgrims were carried in the 'tween decks of, for example, the TELAMON (1) of 1885 on which can be clearly seen the white-painted deadlights that were a distinctive feature of 'Blueys' for years. DARDANUS (2) is another example. By the time they were building the 1906 goal posters the pilgrim accommodation had extended part way into the 'tween decks. Richard believes these ships also carried Chinese to America and were fitted with rice boilers in the forecastle. At a later date the Hadji ships had wooden decks from bow to stern, and space was allocated aft for carrying sheep, which were slaughtered by Muslim butchers.

Memories stirred

Some of the most pleasing features of the correspondence received are the accounts of how the photographs rekindled memories amongst former Blue Funnel officers. Stephen Marsh was senior midshipman on the MENESTHEUS of 1929, which he describes as one of his favourite ships. She had been rebuilt after her war service and, apart from her generators, was in superb condition. In fact, such was her condition with electrical winches, teak and pine decks, that a Cape Cod Canal pilot refused to believe that she had been built in 1929. Coming across the Indian Ocean during a south west monsoon on this

AGAMEMNON (3) of 1929 and her beautiful counter stern.

voyage, the ship's electro-hydraulic steering gear suddenly packed up. MENESTHEUS just fell off into a trough and almost rolled over. Sometime later the chief electrician, having previously phoned the bridge to say that the steering gear was working again, turned up with a piece of black carbon. It was the charred remnants of a monkey which had escaped and walked across the 440 volt busbars of the steering gear. Stephen disagrees with us that the appearance of the AGAMEMNON class was marred by the retention of the counter stern: he asserts that the counters were beautiful.

As a cadet on the bridge of Pacific Steam Navigation's LORETO (6,682/1919), Captain J.C. Morris witnessed the torpedoing of the EURYMEDON by U 29 on 25th September 1940 (page 79). She was torpedoed about amidships on the port side, lost way and settled in the water a little, but remained on an even trim. Some time later another torpedo hit her starboard side, again amidships. The second torpedo probably accounted for most of the casualties, for her passengers and crew were in the process of abandoning ship and the explosion destroyed the starboard lifeboats and their occupants. The EURYMEDON remained afloat and did not sink until the following day. Captain Marsh recalls that most of the escorts had departed earlier that day after reaching the limit of their endurance.

The Scott-Still engines

Following our editorial plea for engineering contributions, we are pleased to include background information kindly supplied by James Pottinger on the design and operation of the highly innovative Scott-Still combined diesel and steam engines installed in the DOLIUS of 1924 and the EURYBATES of 1928.

The two engines in the DOLIUS had four cylinders each, with the diesel section above the piston and steam acting underneath in the same cylinder. The exhaust steam was used to drive a turbo blower which supplied scavenge air to the diesel half of the engine, whilst the exhaust gases from the diesel cylinders were taken to a composite, oil-fired boiler which supplied steam to the steam half of the engine. When the DOLIUS was underway the heat from the exhaust gases was sufficient to generate all the steam needed. Steam was used for starting, reversing and manoeuvring the engines.

EURYBATES (2) of 1928, fitted with a refined version of the Scott-Still steam/diesel engine.

Extensive trials before the acceptance of DOLIUS in 1924 confirmed the anticipated frugal fuel consumption. As an example of her economy, on her sixth voyage from Liverpool to Port Said she used just 8.67 tons of fuel oil per day at an average speed of 11.53 knots. Consumption was 0.353 pounds of fuel per brake horsepower. In a paper read to the Institute of Mechanical Engineers in 1931, Sterry Freeman, Technical Director of Alfred Holt, noted that the machinery gave a saving in fuel consumption of about 20% compared to conventional ships. The disadvantages were the higher initial cost and upkeep.

Two improved and more powerful versions of this engine were fitted in the EURYBATES, these having five single-acting diesel combustion cylinders and two double-acting steam cylinders. Improvements made in the light of experience with the DOLIUS included separating the diesel and steam operations so that the individual cylinders were purely steam or diesel. Scavenging air was delivered by two turbo blowers which were driven by steam raised in two boilers from waste heat from engine exhaust. One, a Scotch type boiler, could also be separately oil fired.

The EURYBATES initially suffered excessive vibration from her engines, to the extent that, at between 90 and 95rpm, the amplitude of the vibration at the ends of the ship was five inches. This was blamed partly on the novel engine design, with five diesel cylinders and two double-acting steam cylinders, and partly on the newly-introduced 'elastic' steel used for the hull. Her *Lloyd's Register* entry included the annotation 'special steel', although in fact it was no more elastic than ordinary steel, but did have a higher yield point which allowed the scantlings to be reduced. This material had been used earlier on the PROMETHEUS and resulted in an additional 250 tons dead weight. After sea trials, it was decided to add one ton balancing weights to two of the main crossheads, and this reduced the vibration to a tolerable level.

Whilst the Scott-Still machinery was efficient, it was complicated in operation, and in 1947 Scotts' Shipbuilding (who had worked with Holts since building the pioneering AGAMEMNON and sisters in the 1860s) carried out a conversion (actually installed by Harland and Wolff at Belfast) in which the steam side of the engine was completely discarded, and the EURYBATES thereafter ran as a pure diesel. In modifying the diesel cylinders, components similar to those fitted to Doxford engines were used. The cost of the conversion was justified by the excellent condition of her hull, and EURYBATES was not sold to breakers until 1958.

Although the Scott-Still engine could hardly be described as a success, many of its novel features became accepted practice in the design of slow-speed diesels.

Elusive tugs

The many small craft owned by Holts seem to have eluded photographers, so we are particularly pleased to reproduce Ian Harmsworth's photograph of the tug HECUBA (54/1945), formerly TID 163. This was taken at Adabiya, Egypt in the Spring of 1948 when HECUBA was attending the berthing of the 1910-built ASCANIUS (3) on one of her last trooping voyages from Mombasa to Liverpool. Ian is scathing about the condition of the troop deck and messing facilities of ASCANIUS at this time, and wonders if she was the last coal-burning troop ship. ASCANIUS was sold in 1949, as in fact was the Sunderland-built HECUBA, which went to French owners as PROVENCE.

Patroclus aground

The work of the Gibsons of St. Mary's means that there is a superb collection of photographs of the grounding of PATROCLUS at Blacknor Point, near Portland Bill on 13th September 1907. As an addition to those reproduced on page 20 of *Blue Funnel Line*, we include others which show the work of removing her cargo.

The first vessels on the scene were the tugs VERNE (42/1896) and QUEEN (56/1906), which used steam pumps in an attempt to reduce some of the fifteen feet of water in the forehold of the PATROCLUS. Two tugs tried to tow her off on the 14th without success, and the tugs VERNE and PETREL (55/1892) then went to fetch barges to take cargo from PATROCLUS.

Lightening PATROCLUS was now seen as the priority, especially as the wheat in numbers 1 and 2 holds kept blocking the pumps. Forty stevedores were sent from Liverpool, and on 15th they arrived together with the INDIA (364/1876), the first of a small fleet of coasters with a draft of less than 13 feet to come alongside. The INDIA took her first cargo of

The tug HECUBA at Adabiya, Egypt in 1948. *[Ian Harmsworth]*

wool, skins, wheat, lead and bananas to Weymouth on the 16th. The bananas, which were being carried as deck cargo, were sent by train to London. However, 300 tons of wheat - presumably already damaged by the water - was jettisoned. Two Admiralty and one Great Western Railway barges arrived on the 16th, along with the salvage steamer LINNET (426/1880). William Robertson's coaster ONYX (557/1903) came alongside on the 17th, the ANNIE (372/1902) and another Liverpool-owned coaster, YORKSHIRE (394/1893), on the 18th, the ONYX and ANNIE taking cargoes into Portland Harbour. The addition of

the Cardiff-registered CELESTE (678/1875) was considered to be sufficient to complete discharge. After much work by divers, an attempt to refloat PATROCLUS was made on the 20th, but failed. The LINNET went to Weymouth to fetch more pumps, and a refloating attempt on the 22nd was successful, resulting in PATROCLUS being beached in Portland Harbour. The successful salvage efforts owed much to a nine-day spell of fine weather and calm seas, as well as to the work of the LINNET and chartered coasters. Photographs of the LINNET and two of the coasters are included here.

Above: PATROCLUS (2) of 1896 aground at Blacknor Point in September 1907. On her port side is the salvage steamer LINNET, with a sailing barge and a large number of small boats alongside, with the steam coaster ANNIE working cargo aft. Another coaster, the INDIA, and another sailing barge can just be seen on the port side. [F. Gibson]

Right: A view of PATROCLUS from the port side. The INDIA is working forward, and a large derrick barge aft. The name of the barge ends in -GALE and from the hull appears to be a cut-down wooden sailing ship: can a reader suggest its identity? [Peter Newall collection]

ANNIE (top)

Ailsa Shipbuilding Co. Ltd., Ayr; 1902, 372gt, 150 feet
C. 2-cyl. by Ross and Duncan, Govan

When chartered to help with the salvage of cargo from the PATROCLUS, ANNIE was officially owned by William Rowland of Liverpool, but he had died four years earlier, and the ANNIE was actually operated by his son, Alfred Rowland. Alfred was determined to move into bigger ships, and in 1911 ANNIE was sold to the Monks family who were expanding their coasting business. It was in the ownership of James Henry Monks (Preston) Ltd. that on 21st September 1924 ANNIE was wrecked in Church Bay, Holyhead whilst on a voyage from Swansea to Liverpool in ballast.

INDIA (middle)

J. Readhead and Co., South Shields; 1876, 364gt, 160 feet
C. 2-cyl. by J. Readhead and Co., South Shields

The iron steamer INDIA was owned in Penzance, and was probably well placed to respond to the call for coasters to lift the cargo of PATROCLUS. She had been built for the Bennett Steam Ship Co. Ltd. of Goole, and ran on their short-sea liner services until 1899, when acquired by John H. Bennetts of Penzance.

The Penzance Bennetts only renamed one of his purchases, but this was given an unusual, and perhaps unique, name: PIVOC (483/1899). The name was formed from the initials of his other ships, the PROGRES (244/1872 - bought from Bazeleys, who feature in this issue), INDIA, VRIL (387/1884), and ORMEROD (474/1885), plus CORNUBIA (420/1890) which actually belonged to another Penzance owner.

In 1913 Bennetts sold the now ageing INDIA to Paulsen and Ivers of Kiel, who gave her the distinctly mundane name NORMAL. She was to continue with these German owners through several changes of company title until 1926 when she went to Estonia as KLARA. Within months she was back in German ownership as IMMENHOF, but on 21st November 1928 she left Nordenham for Kings Lynn and Great Yarmouth with a cargo of phosphate and disappeared. All that was ever found of her was one of her boats, washed ashore at Texel during December.

LINNET (bottom)

Thames Iron Works Shipbuilding and Engineering Co. Ltd., Orchard Shipyard, Millwall; 1880, 426gt, 165 feet
H. 4-cyl. by J. and G. Rennie, Blackfriars, London

This salvage steamer was built as HMS LINNET, a composite, twin-screw, steam gunboat with an impressive armament of two 7 inch guns and three 20 pounders. The Admiralty sold her in April 1904, and after conversion to a salvage steamer LINNET was registered at Liverpool in 1905. Her owners were, to give them their Sunday name, the Liverpool Association for the Protection of Commercial Interests as Respects Wrecked and Damaged Property. No doubt to the lasting relief of their telephonists, this name was abbreviated to the Liverpool Salvage Association. LINNET was sold for breaking up in 1922. *[F. Gibson]*

THE PORT OF WIDNES
Part two
Albert Constable

During the early 1890s there was a rapid decline of throughput at Widnes which cannot be explained by a fall-off in trade. There were still reports of vessels being unable to enter West Bank Dock, and of some having to proceed back downstream to Garston to be unloaded. There were three reasons for these problems: mud, incomplete excavation of the dock, and lack of crane berths.

The amount of silt in the Upper Mersey seems to have increased. Widnes Dock was almost silted up at this time, and a House of Commons Select Committee report suggests that in Liverpool docks 40 tons of silt was dredged each week per acre of water, whilst at Widnes the equivalent figure was 100 tons of silt. In the new West Bank Dock, little provision had been made for dredging. In its earlier state, the method had been to flush the dock at low water from the reservoir, a practice also used in Widnes Dock. Soon after the reopening in 1884, experiments were made with a grab-equipped steam crane mounted on a barge, the mud being loaded into hoppers. Other trials involved suction dredging and a bucket dredger borrowed from the Birmingham Canal Navigation. It can be assumed that suction and bucket dredging proved unsatisfactory, as thereafter grab dredging was used.

The mud problem was greatly aggravated by the need to run off as much as 5 feet of water to enable the coal tip to be used on higher tides. As coal was the major cargo shipped through the docks, the tip was virtually always in use, including at night. Frequently, one tide saw two or three steamers loaded with coal and several more bunkered. A loading rate of 100-200 tons per hour could be achieved by two men on the tip and six trimmers working on the vessel. When capacity permitted, other products were also loaded at the tip, including saltcake and sulphur.

The space occupied by the dredger aggravated the problem of the shortage of berths: whilst a berth was being dredged it could not be used. Only a short length of load-bearing wall was added to the new dock, and over the next 30-40 years timber staging and additional piles at crane berths had to be constructed by maintenance staff as and when labour and finance permitted.

Incomplete excavation of parts of the dock had left the bottom of one arm of the dock 18 inches higher than the cill, a problem which was made worse by the failure to remove the original dock cill during the deepening process.

The difficulties of navigating the Mersey were eased somewhat in 1891 when the Snig Rocks near the Runcorn-Widnes railway bridge were removed as part of the requirements of the Manchester Ship Canal Act. This brought the channel to the north side of the river from Widnes almost to Hale.

New managers, new prosperity

In 1892 an action in the Chancery Court saw Cross replaced as General Manager by a Captain Clanchy. It is not clear whether this change was helpful, but in that year traffic began to increase again from a low of 310,000 tons to reach 380,000 tons in 1894. Then begins another decline, with traffic fluctuating between 250,000 and 300,000 each year until 1902. The reasons for this decline include a price war involving coal which severely reduced shipments, and changes in the chemical industry in which the Leblanc process was giving way to new and better methods of alkali production, a decline which particularly affected the manufacturers of Widnes who were wedded to the old process.

In 1902 Clanchy retired and William Earle, a nephew of John Hutchinson, took over, the change once more being accompanied by growing prosperity. Earle improved facilities, and brought stevedoring under direct control of the estate, it having previously been subcontracted. His improvements more than replaced the traffic lost due to the decline of the local alkali industry, and trade increased in chemicals, sand, stone chippings, setts, macadam, copper, ore and fertiliser, but the main growth was in coal shipments. From 1907 to 1913, the annual tonnage through the dock averaged 550,000 tons, half of which was coal. A major development came when Earle took the dock into a consortium with the Liverpool Lighterage Co. Ltd. and the Denaby Main Colliery Co. Ltd. which bunkered ships lying in the river off Liverpool. This was extremely successful, and saw off competition from coal loaded at Garston and at Brocklebank Dock, despite the geographical advantages of these docks. For a period, steamers of both Cunard and White Star Lines were bunkered from Widnes. Most of the bunker coal was carried in dumb barges towed by tugs. The increased coal traffic required two extra tips at West Bank Dock.

In 1902 the company was taken out of Chancery after 24 years, and John Hutchinson's youngest daughter, Gertrude, assumed control. Although living in London, she became actively involved in the management of the company. It is to her that Earle turned for authority to make the next major improvement, a new entrance with a lock of 160 x 40 feet, capable of taking larger vessels and giving smaller craft a longer period to enter and leave the dock. The dock was also deepened and the cill lowered by 4 feet 6 inches, to the same level as the cill of Liverpool Old Dock.

Mersey flats crowd West Bank Dock, with larger sailing craft behind to the right. To the left are two steamers, the nearer being one of the fleet of tiny coasters owned by Joseph Monks of Warrington, and believed to be the BESSIE (177/1901). *[National Museums and Galleries on Merseyside N89.1505]*

Unfortunately, during work on the lock which began in 1914, the coffer dam failed on several occasions and for weeks at a time the dock was tidal. This had a catastrophic effect: the bunkering trade ceased overnight, so that coal shipments fell from 250,000 tons in 1913 to 20,000 in 1915. General cargo showed a somewhat less steep decline in the same period, from 324,000 to 155,000 tons. To add to West Bank's problems, some of the river sand barges changed to using Widnes Dock.

During the 1920s there was some improvement in traffic, with coal shipments to Ireland and the Isle of Man resuming in 1922. By 1925, a total of 1,975 barges and 372 coasters moved almost 380,000 tons of cargo through the dock, although the balance of traffic had changed so that 54% was river sand, and less than 10% coal. Improvements in the dock included the phasing out of horses for shunting, and the replacement of nine steam cranes by six electric cranes.

Long, slow decline

After 1929 the river sand trade declined, although there was a minor improvement when Widnes Dock closed in 1933. Despite the efforts of Earle's successor, Major G.A. MacDermott, shipments fell to 200,000 tons by the outbreak of the Second World War. Wartime conditions meant a further fall to 100,000 tons per annum

Post-war years saw a growth in the average size of coasters, and there were fewer and fewer days when they could navigate the river and have sufficient water to enter West Bank Dock. By 1936 the number of coasters using the dock had overtaken the number of barges, 565 compared with about 500. In the next eight years, however, the number of coasters declined to 42 per year, although the figure recovered to over 100 in the 1950s when two new trades were secured. One involved movement of asbestos cement corrugated sheets and rainwater goods, an average of 3,750 tons being shipped between 1947 and 1963. Destinations included Northern Ireland and some

Scottish isles, and vessels involved the steamer HOLLYLEAF (301/1917), and motor vessels BENWOOD (341/1936), TORWOOD (264/1930) and GANSEY (401/1944). The second new trade was a groupage service for Irish Steel Holdings Ltd. of Haulbowline, near Cork which averaged 5,100 tons per year between 1952 and 1962, handled in ships such as Tyrrell's HALRONELL (313/1943). This trade had restrictions put on it by H.M. Customs, so that the dock could not build on the experience gained. As a port, Widnes never had full custom's facilities, being covered from Runcorn.

Once the Runcorn-Widnes road bridge opened in July 1961, the end of the dock's trade was just a matter of time. The bridge meant that the cost of transporting goods to industrial south west Lancashire were the same from Widnes and from Runcorn, and the latter had the enormous advantage of being on the Manchester Ship Canal. After 1963, it was only regular cargoes of potash for Fisons Ltd. who had a factory adjacent to West Bank Dock, and large quantities of river sand for Lime-Sand Mortar Ltd. who had a conveyor system to its plant, which enabled facilities to be kept open to serve other occasional users.

The author became Manager and Engineer of the Hutchinson Estate and Dock Company in 1967 and, although a number of initiatives were tried, no new, regular traffic could be attracted. Sand was landed from the motor vessel ROSSENDALE (322/1926) on average seven times on each set of tides, but the vessel's machinery started failing regularly and no replacement was available. The future of the sand trade was already being discussed when a number of the Fison's potash boats missed the tides and had to unload at Runcorn. The die was cast. West Bank Dock closed on 28th October 1970 after the ROSSENDALE had discharged its last cargo. The dock was filled in and the site is now used partly for industrial purposes and - fittingly in view of Widnes' traditions in the sport - partly for rugby pitches.

Looking towards the railway viaduct, the skew arch can be seen to the extreme right behind the crane. The vessels are, left to right, the Dutch coaster HAVIK (478/1941) loading scrap metal, the steamer HOLLYLEAF (301/1917) and Coopers' motor hopper barge ELIZABETH COOPER (227/1937). *[Author's collection]*

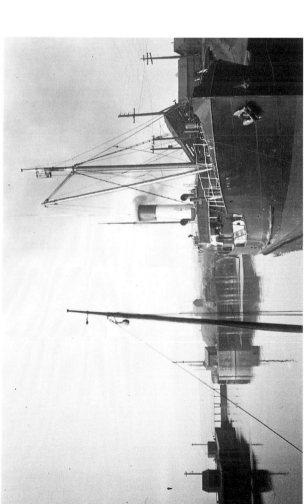

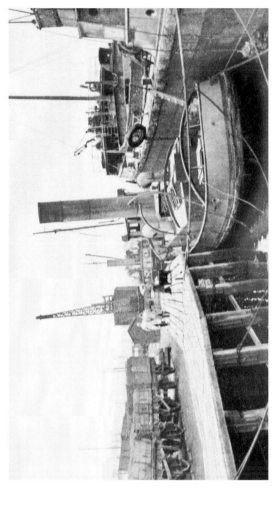

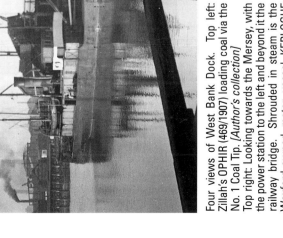

Four views of West Bank Dock. Top left: Zillah's OPHIR (469/1907) loading coal via the No. 1 Coal Tip. *[Author's collection]* Top right: Looking towards the Mersey, with the power station to the left and beyond it the railway bridge. Shrouded in steam is the Wexford-owned motor vessel KERLOGUE

(335/1938) loading asbestos sheets for Ireland, and astern of her is the West Bank Dock dredger and her mud barge. At the right side of the dock, Kelly's motor vessel BALLYEDWARD (552/1950) unloads red ore. The flat with a mast in the left foreground is Coope's' laid-up TAMAR (97/1885), whilst

this section. *[Author's collection]* Bottom right: An unidentified Cooper's tug alongside the old steam hopper ERIC COOPER (959/1893). *[Author's collection]*

Bottom left: The steamer TORPOINT (214/1905) bunkering from the No. 1 Coal Tip with the Dock Offices in the background. Note the condition of the timbers in the foreground: there was never any decking on

one of their concrete barges is sunk to the right. *[Author's collection]*

In July 1960, West Bank Dock looked full. Left to right above are Wm. H. Muller's low air-draught motor vessel SOMME (451/1950) loading bags of Lithaphone for Paris; NORA COOPER (333/1893) unloading sand; Gardner's SAINT RULE (524/1941) in the centre of the dock waiting to unload white sand; the German FRIESENLAND (279/1937) with beech bundles; and with a cargo of pit props the Irish auxiliary DE WADDEN (239/1917), since preserved at Liverpool. No. 1 Coal Tip and the Dock Offices can be seen in the foreground, and Fison's factory in the background.

Another view of the same ships (right) shows why the dock, apparently thriving, lost most of its traffic within a few years: the Runcorn-Widnes road bridge rising in the background. [Both: author's collection]

The Delfzijl-registered DONAU (357/1953) swinging outside West Bank Dock by nudging her nose into the Slag Bank (top left), backing through the lock (top right), and proceeding to her berth (bottom left). In the final shot, pilot Captain Vivian Thomas (with pipe) looks suitably pleased with the manoeuvre. Viv is currently (1999) the only pilot certificated to take vessels up the River Weaver. *[Author's collection]*

Top: Late in 1967, ROSSENDALE (322/1926) unloads sand whilst ZANZIBAR (387/1954) loads 250 tons of bagged fertiliser for Ireland. ZANZIBAR later unloaded this cargo, as there was concern that such cargoes might spread the epidemic of foot-and-mouth disease in the United Kingdom to Ireland. *[Author's collection]*

Middle: NORA COOPER (333/1893) and the Irish motor vessel TYRRONALL (248/1935). *[Author's collection]*

Bottom: As late as 18th November 1968 the soon-to-be-closed West Bank Dock can still boast four vessels. Left to right are the German DINSLAKEN (425/1962) unloading potash, the sand carrier ROSSENDALE (322/1926), the Dutch VEENDAM (397/1958) loading bagged fertiliser, and the German ERIK SEYD II (497/1958) also with potash. *[Author's collection]*

Since publication of the first part of this article, which dealt with the earlier docks at Widnes, Nigel Bowker has supplied photographs of the St. Helens Canal and the Widnes Dock (also known as the Railway Dock).

In the entrance locks and dock of the St. Helens Canal, formerly the Sankey Navigation (above) are, left to right, the wooden motor barge T.H. BURTON (73/1931), and three dumb barges, MARY BURTON, MAY (both in the entrance to the western lock, whose gates are open) and JOHN BURTON (in the entrance to the eastern lock). Burton and Son Ltd. were based at Bromborough Pool, where they also built barges, including T.H. BURTON, for their own fleet.

As the alkali industry developed the St. Helens Canal was widened near its entrance to allow vessels to berth alongside the works (below). Burtons' dumb barge ARTHUR BURTON is in the centre foreground, and their motor barge NORMAN BURTON (74/1927) behind. A well-laden steamer is heading out of the canal with a dumb barge in tow. [Both: Nigel Bowker collection]

Top: Berthed in the St. Helens Canal are the motor barge ISABEL (53/1894) and the steam derrick barge BRENDA (123/1906). ISABEL was built as a steamer, and converted to diesel propulsion in 1920. Owners were the United Alkali Co. Ltd., who subsequently became part of Imperial Chemical Industries Ltd. After almost half a century working alkali traffic between Widnes and Liverpool, ISABEL was sold and sank in Langton Dock, Liverpool in 1952. BRENDA was built by W.J. Yarwood and Sons at Northwich for soap manufacturers William Gossage and Sons Ltd., alongside whose factory she is berthed. Her job was to carry barrels of palm oil from Liverpool Docks to Widnes, sometimes returning with soap for export. Gossages were taken over by Lever Brothers and craft were registered in the new owners name in 1932, but BRENDA still carries Gossage's funnel. In 1946 she was sold to Wadsworth Lighterage and Coaling Co. Ltd., and she was broken up in Canning Dry Dock, Liverpool in 1964. *[Nigel Bowker collection]*

Middle: The No. 1 Coal Tip on the north side of Widnes Dock carries a plate identifying it as LNWR 4086. The dock closed in 1933, and little if any coal went through this dock after coal handling facilities were provided at Garston, but in this view - believed to have been taken around closure - the coal tips look to be in working order, and a coal wagon is poised beyond the far tip. Open wagons with sheeted loads of timber can be seen in the distance. *[Nigel Bowker collection]*

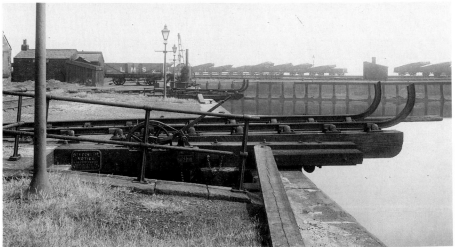

Bottom: Steam cranes on the south side of Widnes Dock. A variety of LMS and LNER open wagons stand on the dockside beyond. The decision of the LNWR to concentrate its traffic on Garston was soon to seal the fate of the dock but, nevertheless, the dock walls appear in better condition than some of those of West Bank Dock, which survived it by over 35 years. *[Nigel Bowker collection]*

Photographer F.H. Howell took a delightful series of photographs of a tug and a string of Mersey flats leaving either the St. Helens Canal or the Railway Dock at Widnes (above) and heading under the Runcorn-Widnes transporter bridge (right). *[John M. Ryan collection]*

SOURCES AND ACKNOWLEDGEMENTS

Photographs are from the collection of John Clarkson unless otherwise credited. We thank all who gave permission for their photographs to be used, and are particularly grateful to David Whiteside and Tony Smith of the World Ship Photo Library; and to Peter Newall, Ivor Rooke, William Schell, George Scott and the museums and institutions listed for help in finding photographs.

In researching captions, sources have included the *Registers* of William Schell and Tony Starke, *Lloyd's Register, Lloyd's Confidential Index, Lloyd's War Losses, Mercantile Navy Lists,* and *Marine News.* Use of the facilities of the World Ship Society's Central Record, the Guildhall Library and Lloyd's Register of Shipping are gratefully acknowledged. Particular thanks also to William Schell and John Bartlett for information, to Heather Fenton for editorial work, and to Marion Clarkson for accountancy services.

John Holt and Co.
Books and articles consulted were *Merchant Adventure* (John Holt & Co. (Liverpool) Ltd., 1951), a pamphlet published by Charles Birchall & Sons Ltd. about 1959, 'Guinea Gulf Line Ltd.' in *Sea Breezes* for April 1961, *A Short History of John Holt & Co. (Liverpool) Ltd. and the Guinea Gulf Line Ltd.* by Peter Davies (Published privately 1965), and *The Trade Makers* by P.N. Davies. (1973). The fleet list was compiled by Geoffrey Holmes and Roy Fenton, with the help of lists by the late Len Gray and another author loaned by the World Ship Society's Fleet List Library.

Every picture tells a story: DRONNING SOPHIE
For records of the SIR GEORGE POLLOCK's passages to New Zealand, see Sir Henry Brett, *White Wings: Fifty Years of Sail in the New Zealand Trade, Vol.II: Founding of the Provinces and Old-Time Shipping. Passenger Ships from 1840 to 1885,* The Brett Printing Company, Auckland, 1928. The loss of the DRONNING SOPHIE is reported in *The Cork Examiner,* Friday, 21st November 1930 and Saturday, 22nd November 1930. Dr. Richard Palmer's comments are taken from personal correspondence.

The port of Widnes
Printed sources are *The St. Helens Railway* by J.M. Tolson (Oakwood Press,1983), *Mersey Flats and Flatmen* by Michael Stammers (Terence Dalton Ltd., Lavenham and National Museums and Galleries on Merseyside, 1993), *A History of Widnes* by G.E. Diggle (Widnes Corporation, Widnes), *History of the Chemical Industry in Widnes* by Hardy (ICI, London), *Canals of North West England* by Charles Hadfield and Gordon Biddle (David and Charles, Newton Abbot, 1970). Unpublished sources include archival material from the Hutchinson Estate and Dock Co. Ltd.; memories and photographs from employees at West Bank Dock and especially Frank Whitby, Dock Master, and Stephen Ronan, Engineer and Manager at Hutchison Estate and Dock Co. Ltd.; and material in the Catalyst Museum, Widnes. Thanks to Nigel Bowker for information on the craft in the photographs on pages 97 and 98.

Boer War transports
Thanks to Bill Laxon, Brian Ingpen and the Ship Society of South Africa.

EVERY PICTURE TELLS A STORY
DRONNING SOPHIE
John Naylon and Gerald Lewis

On the night of Wednesday-Thursday, 19-20th November 1930 a south-east gale brought heavy rain and high seas into Monkstown Bay in the Cove of Cork. Sometime after midnight the ancient wooden coal hulk DRONNING SOPHIE, moored in the bight, sank at her moorings and at dawn only a few feet of her masts were visible. A local diver, Dan Hallissey, was unable to find any sign of the two men who had been on board - the night watchman John Mitchell, of Cottrell's Row, a young single man, and the pump man Thomas Heiher, of Harbour View, married with five young children. The rowing boat used by the men for going to and from the hulk was found on the Thursday morning lying upturned on the Rushbrooke shore. It was concluded that the men were drowned by the boat capsizing as they left the sinking hulk. The cause of the foundering was that the DRONNING SOPHIE had recently been loaded with steam coal for bunkers beyond her usual marks, and water had entered through the treenails which were made of softer wood than her teak hull and had rotted.

The local legend about the hulk was that she had been built in South America and had been a Chilean man-of-war. Her true history was not less colourful.

SIR GEORGE POLLOCK - East Indiaman
The DRONNING SOPHIE had begun life as the country-built full-rigged East Indiaman SIR GEORGE POLLOCK, launched at Moulmein, Burma in 1847 for Engldew of Calcutta. Constructed of teak and sheathed with yellow metal, she measured 630 tons old measurement/553 tons new measurement on dimensions 129.0 x 27.0 x 19.4 feet. Although she was intended for the Indian trade, by the 1850s the demand for passenger ships was diverting vessels to Australia and New Zealand, and we find the SIR GEORGE POLLOCK immediately going out to the Antipodes.

The DRONNING SOPHIE, ex-SIR GEORGE POLLOCK, with Palmers' salvage vessels SHARK, alongside, and PERSEVERANCE, whose bows can just be seen. The picture affords rare photographic evidence of the appearance of the old East Indiamen. The hull looks short, with a great proportion of beam to length, and hardly any sheer. The stern is heavy, the waist short, and the swelling bows are bluff and apple-cheeked. The missing figurehead was probably an upright bust of Sir George. The hulk had been used by the Royal Navy during the First World War and the structures on deck date from that time: a four-bunk sleeping compartment, a galley and a boiler for the pumps and winches. The vessel looks very small, especially for the number of passengers she carried in her early days; the figure standing amidships gives an idea of scale. *[Peter Thomas collection]*

Sir Henry Brett, in *White Wings: Fifty Years of Sail in the New Zealand Trade,* records some of her passages in the 1850s and early '60s, when she was owned by Luscombe of Calcutta and London. In 1851, under Captain Withers, she went out from the Downs to Lyttelton in 117 days with no less than 145 emigrants. In 1859, still under Captain Withers, she took two officers and sixty men of the 65th Regiment (needed in New Zealand because of the insecurity caused by the Maori Wars) plus 47 emigrants out to Auckland from the very Queenstown where she was to meet her end 71 years later. During this passage there were three births and one death on board, and the vessel was pooped in the Southern Ocean, the stern windows being smashed and the after cabin flooded. In 1861, now commanded by Captain Frost, she went from London to Nelson in 121 days. The SIR GEORGE POLLOCK was no clipper.

In the 1870s, when owned by W. Hawkesly of London, she was still classified A1, and she then found a further career under the French flag as the MARIUS before ending her sea-going days owned in Norway as the DRONNING SOPHIE.

Stout service as a coal hulk

Declared a constructive wreck in 1892, the DRONNING SOPHIE was purchased by the Clyde Shipping Company and employed as a coal hulk at Queenstown (Cobh) for the next 38 years - testimony to the durability of those old teak hulls. The India-built 'country' ships had a reputation for combining craftsmanship with superior materials. Fine hardwood teak was strong, imperishable and oily, which preserved the timber, repelled worm and kept the ship tight. The heavily-framed hulls were virtually indestructible; they could not be worn out and could hardly be strained. The DRONNING SOPHIE was 83 years old when she foundered, and even then the fault lay with her treenails and not her teak timbers.

When the Clyde Shipping Company left Cork in 1929 the vessel was sold to the local firm of Colemans for £300. After her loss in 1930 she was raised and broken up by S.R. and R.F. Palmer, shipowners and salvage operators of Ringaskiddy, County Cork (see Gerald Lewis, 'The Palmers of Boston and Ringaskiddy' in *Record* 6 and 7). The reminiscences of Dr. Richard Palmer, a member of the family, give valuable testimony to the construction of the old East Indiamen.

'... for years I broke her up for firewood as we had a pub in Ringaskiddy and there was always a fire in the bar.

All the main knees which supported the decks were cut from the forks of teak trees; these were impossible to split with a sledge and metal wedges. Many of the ribs were likewise shaped from knotty teak and difficult to break. One does not normally associate teak with being knotty; knees were roughly shaped and were about two feet wide with the minimum of preparation.

The teak was of a particular grey colour and it was difficult to find any lengths which were not crossed by dowel pins or bronze fastening bolts which were about an inch and a half in diameter; some were more than four feet long where they entered the frames. The teak was never used for furniture or for making boats for that reason.

Many of the internal frames had iron bolts and these had left a mixture of iron and a cement-like iron oxide residue which rendered the wood such that no saw mill would cut it. Firewood was all that it was fit for. We had a circular saw and cut what we could get to the saw in a manageable piece'.

More on Palmers
David Asprey

Gerald Lewis' pair of articles covering this hotch-potch of a fleet in *Record* 6 and 7 and was really interesting, and the photo selection most impressive. It is worth adding that at least four further vessels passed through the Palmers' hands, though it is unclear whether all of them were with the fleet for long enough to be put into service. There may have been others, but I have only noted those that were tugs or possible salvage vessels.

I am particularly surprised about the omission of TOPMAST No 1, which seems to have been around for many years after the reported end of the Palmers' business in 1955, or is this another case of a vessel hanging on in *Lloyd's Register* long after its demise?

ESTELLA 1890-1897 Wooden tug
O.N. 76769 23g 12n 66.5 x 12.3 x 5.8 feet
C 2-cyl. by M. Paul and Co., Dumbarton; 10NHP.
8.6.1877: Completed by William Denny and Brothers, Dumbarton for Charles Reynardson, Stamford, Lincs as the steam yacht ESTELLA.
9.11.1877: Sold to Peter Denny, Dumbarton.
7.1882: Sold to William Liddell, Glasgow and converted to a tug.
29.11.1882: Sold to Queenstown Towing Co. Ltd., Cork.
26.3.1886: Sold to George Kidston and James Cuthbert (Clyde Shipping Co.), Glasgow.
16.7.1890: Acquired by Frederick Palmer, Boston.
10.5.1897: Foundered off Caistor.

TOPMAST No. 1 1951-1982 Twin-screw salvage vessel
O.N. 163661 106g 35n 85.2 x 18.0 x 9.6 feet
2 x C.2-cyl. by J. Samuel White, East Cowes; 330 IHP.
1902: Built by J. Samuel White, East Cowes for the Admiralty as HMS NETTLE.
27.3.1935: Sold to William Gray, Botley, Hants and renamed TOPMAST No 1.
28.12.1935: Sold to Risdon Beazley Marine Trading Co. Ltd., Southampton.
16.1.1939: Owners became Risdon Beazley Ltd.
29.11.1951: Purchased by Ralph and Richard Palmer, Cork.
c1982: Broken up.

PRIVATEER 1913-1914 Iron paddle tug
O.N. 78447 104g 30n 96.5 x 18.7 x 9.2 feet
L.1-cyl. by G.P. Hepple, North Shields, 65NHP.
1883: Completed by J. and W. Toward, St. Lawrence for William P. Ching, Swansea as PRIVATEER.
16.12.1895: Sold to The Boston Steam Tug Co. Ltd., Boston.
1.7.1913: Purchased by Frederick Palmer, Boston.
23.11.1914: Sold to The Robinson Tug Co. Ltd., Middlesbrough.
5.2.1917: Sold to Charles Duncan and Sons Ltd., Middlesbrough.
14.12.1917: Sold to The Lawson Steam Tugboat Co. Ltd., South Shields.
23.12.1918: Ashore near Boulogne and became a total loss.

EDWARD AURIOL 1917-1918 Launch tug
O.N. 95487 16g 8n 45.7 x 9.5 x 5.0 feet
C.2-cyl. by Edwin Clard and Co., Brimscombe; 18NHP.
1888: Completed by Edwin Clard and Co., Brimscombe for Henry Bloomer, Secretary of the Thames Church Mission, London as EDWARD AURIOL.
31.8.1891: Sold to the Thames Church Mission, London.
31.4.1904: Transferred to Thames Church Mission and Missions to Seamen.
27.2.1911: Sold to William Hepworth, Hull.

15.3.1913: Sold to The Tinsley Park Colliery Co. Ltd., Sheffield.
10.1.1917: Sold to Thomas H. Cade, Torksey.
10.3.1917: Purchased by Frederick Palmer, Boston.
13.6.1918: Sold to Osbourne Graham and Co. Ltd., Sunderland.
21.5.1920: Sold to Joseph Gunn, North Shields.
5.7.1920: Sold to Charles Minto, North Shields.
29.9.1924: Sold to George Harrison, Gateshead.
15.3.1926: Sold to John Devlin junior, Gateshead.
13.6.1930: Registry closed, vessel broken up.

Having been shown David's additions, Gerald Lewis contacted Richard Palmer, who had heard vaguely of the PRIVATEER, but had no knowledge of the other tugs being in his family's ownership. He found it difficult to believe that his family would purchase the TOPMAST No 1 as late as 1951 as they were definitely running the business down. Richard Palmer suggests that the Palmers may have been listed as nominal owners of the vessel on behalf of Haulbowline Industries at Passage West, Cork, who purchased vessels for breaking up to supply scrap to a local steelworks.

Above: The paddle tug PRIVATEER off Packhorse Quay, Boston. The tower of St. Botolph's Church - the 'Boston Stump' - is in the background. The town bridge can be seen behind the foremast of the PRIVATEER. *[Local Studies Collection Lincoln Central Library, by courtesy of Lincolnshire County Council Educational and Cultural Services Directorate]*

Opposite top: PRIVATEER towing the Norwegian URANIA (1,688/1891) out of Boston Dock on 3rd June 1904. The steel barque had arrived from Rosario on 30th April with 2,750 tons of linseed for a local company. During her protracted stay at Boston, her original crew left her, and the local paper reported that when she left for her home port of Christiansand with 1,000

tons of coal, it was with a crew signed on from the Scandinavian Seaman's Home at Hull. Note the URANIA's painted ports. *[Local Studies Collection Boston Library, by courtesy of Lincolnshire County Council Educational and Cultural Services Directorate]*

Ian Wilson has provided further information on the original service of the steamer DURAS, featured in the article on Palmers of Boston and Ringaskiddy in *Record* 7, and seen again right. Her owners, the Galway Bay Steamboat Co. Ltd., began steamer sailings on Galway Bay in 1872 with the paddler CITIE OF THE TRIBES (117/1872). On the strength of financial assistance given by the Congested Districts Board, the company took delivery of the DURAS in 1893. She made three sailings a week from Galway to the Aran Islands and during summers from 1898 made thrice weekly sailings on alternate days to Ballyvaughan in County Clare. From there a coach service connected with the West Clare Railway at Ennistymon. In 1912 the DURAS was replaced on these services by the DUN AENGUS (234/1912), which continued until 1958.

The foregoing is derived from Patrick Flanagan's *Transport in Ireland* 1880-1910 (Transport Research Associates, 1969), which includes several other photographs of DURAS amongst the Aran Islands, all of them showing her - as she is here - proudly flying a name pennant from her foremast.

A late afternoon view of Table Bay in March 1900 showing the congestion at Cape Town (above). Sailing ships as usual had relatively low priority and many would spend weeks in the roadstead waiting to offload their cargo. During the winter months, especially May to July, this was not a comfortable nor safe place to be with no escape from the northwest gales which blew across the bay from left to right of the photograph. [Cape Archives S82/S83]

MONTEAGLE (below)
Palmers Shipbuilding and Iron Co. Ltd., Jarrow 1899, 5,498gt, 445 feet
Two T. 3-cyl. by Palmers Shipbuilding and Iron Co. Ltd., Jarrow
A typical scene of chaos in Cape Town's nearly completed outer harbour, the Victoria Basin. The MONTEAGLE was one of two ships built by Palmers for the Elder Dempster Avonmouth-Montreal service. Essentially a cargo ship with limited passenger accommodation, she was chartered for Boer War service as Transport No. 87 and, after one round trip to the Cape with troops, she carried horses from New Orleans and Austrian remounts from Fiume to South Africa. In 1903 the Canadian Pacific Railway Company entered the North Atlantic trade and bought Elder Dempster's Canadian services, including MONTEAGLE and fourteen other vessels. Fitted with 97 cabin class berths she was placed on the CPR Pacific service as a rather incongruous running mate to EMPRESS OF RUSSIA and EMPRESS OF ASIA. After a brief spell as an Indian troopship, she returned to the trans-Pacific run in 1915 and was scrapped at Blyth in 1926. [Martin Leendertz Collection S.A. Library]

RANEE (opposite page bottom)
Charles Connell and Co. Ltd., Glasgow 1899, 5,660gt, 420 feet
T. 3-cyl. by Dunsmuir and Jackson, Glasgow
Seen at sunset in Table Bay, RANEE was chartered by the British Government from October 1899 to January 1902. She carried troops and horses - the horse stalls are clearly visible on deck in the photograph. Owned by the Asiatic Steam Navigation Co. Ltd., she and her sisters RAJAH and RAJPUT were considerably larger than anything built for the company so far and were also the first ships not to come from Harland and Wolff. The star emblem on the house flag and the connection with Harland and Wolff is evidence of a close involvement with the Ismay family of White Star Line fame. Bruce Ismay, in fact, was chairman of Asiatic Steam from 1907 until 1934. The company traded mainly as a cargo and coolie carrier around the Indian subcontinent with Calcutta as its main base. The three Rs survived the First World War and were disposed of in the early 1920s. RANEE became the Greek THEODORIS and was sold for scrap at Bilbao in 1932. [Cape Archives E8861]

BOER WAR TRANSPORTS
Peter Newall

When the Peace of Vereeniging was signed on 31st May 1902 the Anglo-Boer War was finally over. For the British public there was little to celebrate. This war which should have been over 'by teatime' dragged on for over two and a half years and cost £200 million and 20,000 British lives. The lack of planning by the anonymous bureaucrats of Whitehall and the numerous blunders of the Army generals had been the source of great embarrassment for the nation and added considerably to the final tally of those wounded and killed. With the deaths of 28,000 Boer women and children and 14,000 Africans in the infamous concentration camps, the image of Britain abroad was also dented forever.

The logistical problems of fighting a war so far from home were horrendous. Between July 1899 and December 1902 chartered ships carried 609,400 troops to and from South Africa at a total cost of £14.7 million. In addition, over a quarter of a million horses and one hundred thousand mules were shipped to the battle zone. In South Africa, Cape Town was the only harbour which was capable of landing troops and equipment directly from large ships onto the quayside and vessels had to wait weeks in the roadstead before entering the harbour. At Port Elizabeth, East London and Durban sand bars and shallow waters meant that equipment and men had to be offloaded into barges and tenders.

For ship enthusiasts like Martin Leendertz in Cape Town, however, this was a unique opportunity to see a multitude of vessels, some of which were the most famous ships of the day. To co-incide with the centenary of the outbreak of the Anglo-Boer War on 11th October 1899, this article shows a few of the vessels which were used during the campaign.

INDIAN TROOPERS

NUBIA (above)

Caird and Co. Ltd., Greenock; 1895, 5,914gt, 430 feet

T. 3-cyl. by Caird and Co. Ltd., Greenock

Most Boer War troop transports had numbers painted on their sides although many of these changed between 1899 and 1902. Here are two with No. 1 which appears on at least six different vessels.

NUBIA was among the first Boer War troopships to be chartered and on her inaugural voyage south in October 1899 she carried 1,665 men, the largest number of the war so far. Built for P and O's intermediate service, she and her sisters SIMLA and MALTA carried 152 first and second class passengers in peacetime guise. In 1894 the Admiralty decided to charter ships when required instead of replacing their own twenty-eight year old troopships. P and O

was awarded the first six-month contract during the Indian trooping season of 1894/5 and NUBIA was among a group of P and O ships which were also used as troopers when the need arose. Later in the Boer War she was converted into a hospital ship and subsequently returned to her owners in September 1903. On a voyage from Colombo to Shanghai, she was wrecked just north of Colombo on 20th June 1915. *[Peter Newall Collection]*

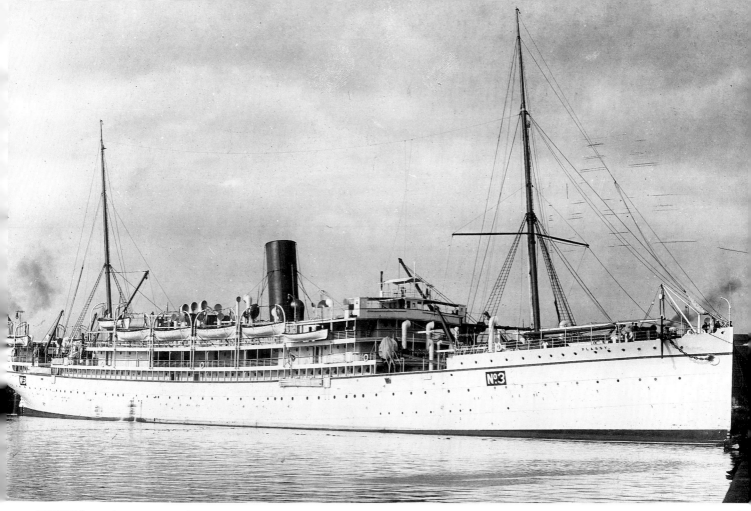

DUNERA (opposite page bottom)
A. and J. Inglis Ltd., Pointhouse; 1891, 5,413gt, 425 feet
T. 3-cyl. by A. and J. Inglis Ltd., Pointhouse
P and O's great rival in India, the British India Steam Navigation Co. Ltd. also benefited from the new troopship chartering arrangements of 1894 and their relatively new three-masted DUNERA and DILWARA were used almost exclusively on peacetime trooping duties. Transferred from Indian service in November 1899 DUNERA was used for the next two years mainly as a Boer War infantry hospital ship. In 1915 after the P and O/British India amalgamation DUNERA and DILWARA were transferred to the Bombay-Japan mail service and in 1922, they were sold to Chinese breakers. *[Martin Leendertz Collection S.A. Library]*

PLASSY (above)
Caird and Co. Ltd., Greenock; 1901; 7,405gt, 450 feet
Two T. 3-cyl. by Caird and Co. Ltd., Greenock
This handsome ship was built for P and O towards the end of the Boer War and was used between December 1901 and September 1902 as an Indian and Boer War troop transport. Her sisters were ASSAYE and SOBRAON and although designed for the intermediate passenger service she was used almost exclusively as a troopship. In 1906 she received severe damage following a collision with F.H. Powell's MASTERFUL (1,794/1905) whilst berthed at Southampton. During the First World War she became the naval hospital ship HMHS PLASSY and was one of the hospital ships anchored in the Firth of Forth to receive casualties during the Battle of Jutland. In 1924 she was broken up at Genoa. *[Peter Newall Collection]*

SYRIA (below)
Alexander Stephen and Sons Ltd., Glasgow; 1901, 6,660gt, 450 feet
Two T.3-cyl. by Alexander Stephen and Sons Ltd., Glasgow
Between 1901 and 1905, P and O took delivery of five intermediate/troopships all with names beginning S. SYRIA was the third in this series of rather functional-looking ships with a single enclosed promenade deck. In Boer War service for only nine months, she carried over 9,000 troops to and from South Africa. After a fairly uneventful career, she too was sold to Italian breakers in 1924. *[Peter Newall Collection]*

HORSES AND MEN

As well as troop transports, many ships were fitted out as cavalry transports whilst others carried only mules or horses. With the guerrilla tactics of the Boers the British had to chase the enemy over long distances and this required large numbers of horses. As the war progressed the death toll among the animals was appalling. Poor planning meant that many were sent to the front without any rest from the strenuous sea journey and succumbed to disease or starvation. Whilst 75,000 horses left England with the cavalry, only 2,400 returned. In total, over a quarter of a million horses and one hundred thousand mules were sent to South Africa between 1899 and 1902.

WINIFREDIAN (top)
Harland and Wolff Ltd., Belfast; 1899, 10,405gt; 552 feet
T. 3-cyl. by Harland and Wolff Ltd., Belfast
WINIFREDIAN was less than six months old when she was sent to South Africa for the first of two voyages as a cavalry transport. Designed for the Frederick Leyland and Co. Ltd. Liverpool-Boston service, she and her sister DEVONIAN were large cargo carriers with accommodation for 135 first class passengers. She also had 'tween deck space for the carriage of live cattle and this made her ideal as a cavalry transport. In 1901, the International Navigation Company of New Jersey - owners of the Red Star and American Lines - acquired Leyland Line and the following year the entire group came under the control of the financier J. Pierpoint Morgan and was reformed as the International Mercantile Marine Co. (IMM). The company continued to operate, however, as Leyland Line. The fleet was badly depleted after the First World War with twenty-two ships sunk by German submarines - WINIFREDIAN and BOHEMIAN were the only passenger ships to survive the war. Apart from a brief spell with Red Star Line, WINIFREDIAN spent most of her career on the Liverpool-Boston service and in 1929 was scrapped in Italy.
[Martin Leendertz Collection S.A. Library]

ATLANTIAN (above)
Armstrong, Whitworth and Co. Ltd., Newcastle-upon-Tyne, 1899, 9,355gt, 482 feet
Two T.3-cyl. by Wallsend Slipway Co. Ltd., Newcastle-upon-Tyne
Despite the -IAN end to her name ATLANTIAN was built for the West India and Pacific Steamship Co. of Liverpool which had been founded in 1863. Like the distinctive T. and J. Harrison four-masted cotton traders this twin-screw ship was also designed for the US Gulf cotton business. Completed in September, she arrived at Cape Town on December 28, 1899 with 500 men and 376 horses. Three days later the company merged with Leyland Line to form a new company Frederick Leyland and Co. (1900) Ltd. which would operate the former West India and Pacific and Leyland routes to the US Gulf ports, Caribbean and Northern USA. The following year the architect of the

scheme, John Ellerman, paved the way for the eventual take-over of Leyland by IMM. In June 1918 ATLANTIAN was torpedoed in the North Atlantic by a German submarine whilst on a voyage from Galveston to Liverpool with a cargo of cotton. *[Martin Leendertz Collection S.A. Library]*

MANHATTAN (opposite page top)
Harland and Wolff Ltd., Belfast; 1898, 8,004gt, 491 feet
Two T.3-cyl. by Fawcett, Preston and Co., Liverpool
MANHATTAN had been completed as a cargo ship for the Atlantic Transport Line but was transferred to the ATL subsidiary National Line for service between London and New York. The National Steam Navigation Co. Ltd. was another Liverpool firm which had been founded in 1863 and, after a period a great success in the 1870s as a North Atlantic passenger line, the

company steadily declined. By 1896 when they were taken over by ATL they were already a spent force. MANHATTAN was chartered as a cavalry transport from January 1900 to June 1902 and cost the British tax payer £270,937. During that period she carried over 6,000 men and 4,000 horses. Originally built with a flush deck, to accommodate horses she was fitted with an extra deck which was covered with removable boards (middle photograph). After seven trooping voyages to South Africa including one from Australia, MANHATTAN returned to her owners who were also swallowed up by IMM. In 1927 she was sent to Italy for demolition. [Peter Newall Collection]

DRAYTON GRANGE (bottom)
Workman, Clark and Co. Ltd., Belfast; 1901, 6,592gt, 451 feet
T. 3-cyl. by Workman, Clark and Co. Ltd., Belfast
Houlder Bros. and Co. Ltd. became a major player in the Boer War when they were appointed by the Remount Department of the War Office to look after the chartering arrangements for the carriage of mules and horses from Australia, Argentina, Canada and the United States to South Africa. Most of the 100,000 mules shipped to South Africa were loaded at New Orleans as well as over 80,000 horses, whilst 26,000 horses came from Argentina. DRAYTON GRANGE was chartered for a single voyage from New Orleans and is seen at Cape Town in February 1902 after arriving with 910 horses. Sold in 1912 to the New Zealand Shipping Co. Ltd. and renamed TYRONE, she was sold again shortly afterwards to the Union Steamship Co. of New Zealand Ltd. for use on the Australia-North America Pacific coast service. Before she was able to take position on her new route, however, she was wrecked on the coast of New Zealand in September 1913. [Martin Leendertz Collection S.A. Library]

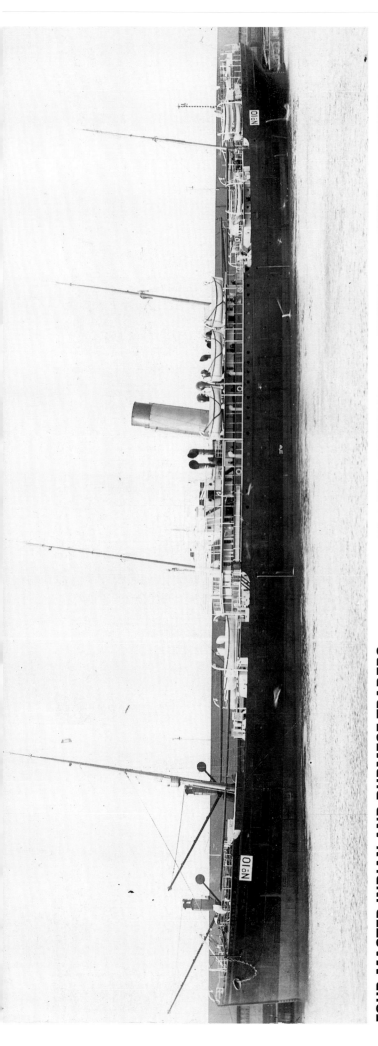

FOUR-MASTED INDIAN AND BURMESE TRADERS

STAFFORDSHIRE (above)
Harland and Wolff Ltd., Belfast; 1894, 6,005gt, 456 feet

Two T. 3-cyl. by Harland and Wolff Ltd., Belfast

A number of Bibby Line ships were chartered during the Boer War including STAFFORDSHIRE which was used as a troopship in the second half of 1902. Completed in 1894 she was the first of the Bibby four-masters to have the mainmast on the boat deck just forward of the bridge. She operated on the Liverpool-Rangoon service with accommodation for 145 first class passengers and when an improved version, DERBYSHIRE, arrived in 1897 the company was able to increase the frequency of Burma sailings to once every three weeks. In 1912 she was sold to the newly formed Cie. de Nav. Sud Atlantique, Bordeaux and renamed SAMARA. Joining her on the new service were a number of well-known liners including the former Castle Line TINTAGEL CASTLE and AVONDALE CASTLE. In 1922 she was scrapped. *[Peter Newall Collection]*

CITY OF CAMBRIDGE (right)
Workman, Clark and Co. Ltd., Belfast; 1882, 3,844gt, 400 feet

C. 2-cyl. by J. and J. Thomson, Glasgow

Seen leaving Cape Town with an enormous ensign, CITY OF CAMBRIDGE was one of the older troopships used during the war and was chartered for almost two years from October 1899. She was one of a large fleet owned by George Smith and Sons, which became City Line Ltd. in 1890. After the opening of the Suez Canal in 1869, the company ordered a number of steamers and started a regular service between Glasgow and Bombay, which was highly successful. In August 1901 City Line was taken over by John Ellerman. After her Boer War service CITY OF CAMBRIDGE was transferred to the Mediterranean service of Papayanni and Co. and on a voyage from Alexandria to Liverpool in July 1917 she was torpedoed and sunk by a German submarine off the coast of Algeria. *[Peter Newall Collection]*

FORGOTTEN LINES

DUKE OF NORFOLK (above)

R. and W. Hawthorn, Leslie and Co. Ltd., Newcastle-upon-Tyne; 1889, 3,819gt, 350 feet

T. 3-cyl. by R. and W. Hawthorn, Leslie and Co. Ltd., Newcastle-upon-Tyne

DUKE OF DEVONSHIRE and two other ships for the Eastern Steamship Company were the first vessels built by the Barrow Shipbuilding Company. Established in 1871 to operate a service between England and Calcutta, Ducal Line as it was commonly known was later controlled by the leading London shipbroker J. B. Westray and Company. In the latter part of the 19th century services were changed from India to Australia and New Zealand and in 1898 the company bought three second-hand vessels from the Shire Line including NAIRNSHIRE which was renamed DUKE OF NORFOLK and is seen here entering Cape Town during the Boer War. The company was wound up in 1905 and the DUKE OF NORFOLK was sold to German owners as MARCELLUS. In 1914, she foundered in a gale off Ushant as the Greek PERICLES.
[Martin Leendertz Collection S.A. Library]

WAKOOL (below)

Sunderland Shipbuilding and Co. Ltd., Sunderland; 1898, 5,004gt, 400 feet

T. 3-cyl. by North Eastern Marine Co. Ltd., Newcastle-upon-Tyne

The Danish born Wilhelm Lund built up a successful emigrant service to Australia with his line which was incorporated into a limited company in 1904 as the Blue Anchor Line Ltd. WAKOOL was one of three new ships built for the company by the Sunderland yard between 1896 and 1899. She was chartered for the entire Boer War from October 1899 to November 1902 as a cavalry and infantry transport. After the mysterious disappearance of the year-old WARATAH in 1909 the fleet was taken over by P and O. With the arrival of the B class Australian emigrant ships, WAKOOL was sold in 1914 to a Japanese company and renamed KWANTO MARU. In 1917 she was bought by the French Government as LE MYRE DE VILLIERS and two years later ended up with Brabant et Provost. In 1923 she was sold to breakers at La Spezia.
[Martin Leendertz Collection S.A. Library]

TRIUMPH AND TRAGEDY

MARIPOSA (right and below)
J. L. Thompson and Sons Ltd., Sunderland;
1900, 4,656gt, 390 feet
T. 3-cyl. by Blair and Co. Ltd., Stockton
With so many ships coming and going during the Boer War and a dangerous coastline it is surprising how few vessels came to grief during this period. The MARIPOSA had only been completed in January and was the largest in the cargo ship fleet of the New York shipowner T. Hogan and Sons when she caught fire at Port Elizabeth in May 1900. Beached, she was refloated three months later and towed to East London where she was declared a constructive total loss. She was, however, repaired and sold in 1904 to the Lingham Timber and Trading Co. and renamed PINEWOOD. After a year she was bought by J. Herron and Co.'s Lord Line as LORD STANLEY. In December 1917 as the Italian ATTUALITA she was torpedoed in the Mediterranean by a German submarine.
[Peter Newall Collection]

HERMES (middle)
John Blumer and Co., Sunderland; 1899,
3,400gt, 350 feet
T.3-cyl. by J. Dickinson and Sons Ltd.,
Sunderland
Another relatively new ship, which did not have a second chance, belonged to Robert Houston's British and South American Steam Navigation Co. Ltd. HERMES was one of a series of cargo ships built for the company in the late 1890s and on 12th May 1901 she arrived in Table Bay with a large consignment of forage from Argentina. Fodder was imported because the dry conditions in the interior could not support grazing for so many horses. With the tiny harbour full she anchored in the roadstead. During the night one of the notorious Cape northwesterly gales sprang up and, with her anchors dragging, she was blown ashore. Only five days before, the Union-Castle liner TANTALLON CASTLE was wrecked on the nearby Robben Island. Two lives were lost when one of the lifeboats overturned. A constructive total loss, the remains of her boilers can still be seen. *[Cape Archives E8855]*

MANILA (bottom)
Caird and Co. Ltd., Greenock; 1892, 4,210gt,
385 feet
T. 3-cyl. by Caird and Co. Ltd., Greenock
Unable to cope with the thousands of Boer prisoners-of-war, the British authorities initially sent them to St. Helena. Among those sent to that remote island was the Boer leader General Cronje whom many of Boer descent still blame for the ignominious surrender of his entire force in 1900. As the

numbers increased, two prison camps were established on Ceylon and over 3,000 were also sent to Bermuda where they were quartered on five different islands. MANILA was one of the ships used to transport the prisoners to Bermuda. Built for P and O's

India and Far East intermediate service she was chartered as an infantry transport during the Boer War. In 1910 she was sold to Italian owners and was scrapped in 1925 as BRACCIANO. *[National Maritime Museum 58/3871]*

AVOCA (top)
William Denny and Bros., Dumbarton; 1891,
5,324gt, 420 feet
Q. 4-cyl. by Denny and Co., Dumbarton
The great tragedy of the Boer War was the large unnecessary loss of life among soldiers and inmates of the concentration camps through poor hygiene. Sixty percent of the British troops who perished in South Africa died of disease - among officers the figure was only 20%. A number of hospital ships were employed during the war including AVOCA, the first transport to be chartered by the British Government in July 1899. Built for the British India Steam Navigation Co. Ltd. in 1891, she was one of three similar sisters designed for the mail

service to Australia and had a very colourful career. Prior to the Boer War, she had been chartered by Compañía Trasatlántica, Barcelona as a troopship to Cuba and renamed SAN FERNANDO. In 1907 she was sold to the A/S Det Østasiatiske Kompagni (East Asiatic Co.), Copenhagen for service in the Caribbean as ATLANTA. Laid up she was bought for an unsuccessful service between Hamburg and New York in 1908 and reverted to AVOCA. Subsequently named URANIUM, she spent the last year of her career with Cunard Line as FELTRIA before being torpedoed off the coast of Ireland with the loss of forty-five lives in May 1917. *[Peter Newall Collection]*

EARLY CELEBRATIONS
On 1st September 1900, after the defeat of the Boers by the armies of Lord Roberts and General Sir Redvers Buller, the Transvaal Republic became the British colony of Transvaal. On 24th October 1900 Buller left Cape Town on DUNVEGAN CASTLE for a hero's welcome in England. The scene above shows the celebration in the Victoria Basin prior to his departure. Bedecked in flags are the paddle tug JOHN PATTERSON (99/1882), the two-funnelled tug T. E. FULLER (399/1898), Transport No.3 DILWARA and another transport. The British triumph was short-lived, however, as a vicious guerrilla war ensued which extended the war for another year and a half.

THE KING ORRY OF 1946
John Shepherd

Whilst spending the summer of 1975 sailing as a seasonal purser on the Isle of Man Steam Packet Company's KING ORRY, I came across a complete set of her deck logs which were quietly rotting away in the forecastle. As it was likely that these logs would have been destroyed in a quayside bonfire before the KING ORRY went to the breakers' yard, I took them home with me and spent part of the next ten years analysing all the available information contained in them. This article is a short précis of my analysis. The reader could gain the impression that the KING ORRY's career was a succession of storms and mishaps; this is patently not so and it should be remembered that about 98% of the KING ORRY's sailings were pure routine. It is, however, the storms and the mishaps which provide some of the interest.

The KING ORRY of 1946 was the fourth vessel to carry the name in the Isle of Man Steam Packet Company's fleet. Her predecessor, built in 1913, was lost at Dunkirk on 30th May 1940. The new KING ORRY was the first of six generally similar steamers built for the company between 1946 and 1955. The last of the class, the MANXMAN, is lying in a sad and neglected state at the Pallion Yard at Sunderland.

The KING ORRY's principal details were:
Steel twin-screw steamer, geared turbines
Official number: 165282 Signal letters: G M J M
Built and engined: Cammell Laird and Co. Ltd., Birkenhead, yard no 1169
Gross tonnage: 2,485 Speed: 21 knots
Overall length: 345.9ft Breadth: 47.01ft

The keel of the KING ORRY was laid on 1st February 1945, and she was launched by Mrs Alexander Robertson, wife of the chairman of the Steam Packet Company, on 22nd November 1945. The new steamer arrived in Douglas on her way to the Firth of Clyde for sea trials on 12th April 1946. At that time Captain Jack Ronan was a seaman on board the MONA'S ISLE (built in 1906 as the ONWARD), and he recalls the KING ORRY's arrival: *"Probably the most vivid and exciting moment of that time was when the new KING ORRY arrived from Cammell Laird in April 1946. The lads from the 'Isle' crossed the King Edward Pier to have a look at this new and beautiful ship. We were still in the aftermath of war with its grim austerities and - I do not exaggerate - it was the most wonderful experience ever for a young lad new to the sea to perceive all those modern furnishings and gadgets, the magic of which in later life, when looking over new ships (and there were many) was never quite recaptured."*

The KING ORRY's maiden voyage in company service took place on Maundy Thursday 18th April 1946, when she left Prince's Stage, Liverpool, at 10.57 and arrived at Douglas at 14.35. Between that April day in 1946 and 31st August 1975, the KING ORRY made 7,412 crossings of the Irish Sea for the Isle of Man Steam Packet Company. She steamed 516,770 miles and carried 3,325,500 passengers. This total of 7,412 crossings breaks down as follows:

KING ORRY in 'as-built' form during 1946, with no docking or 'flying' bridge and a cravat cowl on her funnel.

[Raymond Brandreth collection]

Above: The first class dining saloon.
[*Stewart Bale*]

Below: The first class main lounge.
[*Stewart Bale*]

Douglas and Liverpool on winter service: 2,709 (36.55%)
Douglas and Liverpool on summer service: 2,161 (29.15%)
Douglas and Fleetwood: 817 (11.02%)
Douglas and Ardrossan: 374 (5.05%)
Douglas and Belfast: 284 (3.83%)
Douglas and Dublin: 268 (3.62%)
Douglas and Llandudno: 225 (3.03%)
Liverpool and Llandudno: 190 (2.56%)
Douglas and Heysham: 125 (1.69%)

The remaining 259 crossings were 'light' positioning sailings, or when the KING ORRY was running for shelter when gales made conditions difficult at Douglas. The term 'winter' applies to the period of single daily sailings, usually from the second Monday in September until the Whitsun week-end.

In the 169-year history of the Isle of Man Steam Packet Company, no vessel has worked as hard or served the company more reliably than the KING ORRY. Whilst most of the Manx fleet spent nine months of the year laid up, the KING ORRY maintained the winter sailings from 1946 until 1961 with the exception of the winter of 1951/52, when she herself took a well-earned break. Some of the more interesting or unusual events in the KING ORRY's career are described below.

Tuesday, 11th November 1947
The KING ORRY left Douglas for Liverpool at 09.04. Captain W. Cubbin was in command and Mr T.E. Cain was mate. It was a stormy day with a full south-westerly gale, a heavy sea running, heavy showers and moderate visibility. At 10.45 a man was sighted in the water and the KING ORRY was stopped. The motor lifeboat was lowered under the command of the second officer at 11.00 and the man was picked up at 11.30. The boat was hoisted, but a second man was then sighted; the boat was lowered again and he was picked up at 12.40. Again the boat was hoisted and the KING ORRY steamed round in the vicinity before proceeding on passage at 13.15. The survivors were Capt. T. Adamson and able seaman N.E. Burns from the motor schooner ELLIE PARK which had foundered on passage from Douglas to Connah's Quay.

Friday, 23rd June 1950
The KING ORRY took a charter sailing from Belfast to Rothesay on the Isle of Bute. She left Belfast at 08.08, took at pilot at Cumbrae, and was alongside Rothesay Pier at 12.55. This was the farthest north that the KING ORRY ever sailed. Leaving Rothesay at 18.34, the return passage to Belfast was made in 4 hours 59 minutes.

Wednesday, 5th July 1950
The KING ORRY visited Peel for the first time on Tuesday 4th July and arrived alongside the breakwater at 18.10 in preparation for the Tynwald Fair Day excursion to Belfast the following day. Leaving Peel at 09.45, she crossed to Belfast in 3 hours 20 minutes and was back in Peel at 21.25 after a passage of 3 hours 17 minutes. The weather was perfect, north-easterly force 1, smooth sea and good visibility

Saturday, 16th September 1950
Leaving Fleetwood for Douglas at 15.31, the KING ORRY encountered south-south-east force 8 conditions. Douglas harbour was unapproachable and so she went north to Ramsey Bay for shelter and anchored at 19.22. Her unfortunate passengers had to spend the night on board, and by morning the wind was round to west-south-west and blowing force 9. The KING ORRY's anchor was aweigh at 07.35 and it took her 1 hour 55 minutes to cover the fifteen miles to the South Edward Pier at Douglas where she arrived at 09.30 on Sunday 17th September - 17 hours and 59 minutes after leaving Fleetwood. This was a personal record for the KING ORRY but not for the crossing - the RUSHEN CASTLE was at sea for 71 hours on passage between Fleetwood and Peel in January 1940.

Wednesday, 23rd May 1951
With Captain Oscar Taylor as master and Mr A.W.G. Kissack as mate, the KING ORRY left North Prince's Stage at 15.31, passed the Rock Light at 15.39, the Mersey Bar at 16.15 and was abeam Douglas Head at 18.41. She was alongside the South Edward Pier at 18.49, 3 hours 18 minutes after leaving Liverpool and having completed her fastest ever passage between Liverpool and Douglas.

Sunday, 14th October 1951
The KING ORRY stocked up with galley and heating coal at Liverpool for a long winter lay-up and sailed at 05.23 for Barrow where she berthed alongside the LADY OF MANN at 12.10 in the Devonshire Dock. It was the KING ORRY's first long break since entering service five-and-a-half years earlier, and she would not get another one until the autumn of 1962 when the new car ferry MANX MAID superseded her on the winter service.

Saturday, 2nd August 1952
Leaving Liverpool at 00.27, the KING ORRY had 2,160 passengers on board; on the return sailing from Douglas at 06.15 she carried 1,900. At 10.50 she sailed from Liverpool again with her full complement of 2,160 passengers, and the day was rounded off with the 16.00 Douglas to Fleetwood sailing with 1,440 passengers: a total of 7,660 passengers in 24 hours.

Thursday, 7th August 1952
The KING ORRY steamed from Prince's Stage to Douglas Head in 3 hours 08 minutes (15.35-18.43), but after a slight berthing delay she was not alongside the Edward Pier until 18.54, giving an overall passage time of 3 hours 19 minutes. These fast passages compare very favourably with today's 'fast-craft', which rarely complete the Liverpool and Douglas crossing, berth to berth, in under three hours.

Saturday, 31st January 1953
On Thursday 29th January, Captain Albert Whiteway, who brought the KING ORRY out in 1946, made his last trip as master of the vessel. Captain P.J. 'Ginger' Bridson took over the next day, taking the steamer to Liverpool. On Saturday 31st January the Irish Sea produced the worst conditions the KING ORRY ever encountered. She left

KING ORRY blowing her powerful triple-chime whistle whilst approaching Prince's Landing Stage on 28th April 1951. *[Keith P. Lewis]*

Liverpool at 10.55 with 120 passengers on board and after passing the Rock Light met the full force of a north-north-west force 11 storm. This quickly deteriorated into a full force 12 with frequent sleet squalls and a heavy sea. The KING ORRY passed the inward bound MONA'S QUEEN at 12.30, and speed was then reduced to about six knots for the passage to Douglas, although she was hove-to for over three hours at one stage. It will be recalled that it was on this stormy day that the PRINCESS VICTORIA foundered in the North Channel. The KING ORRY took 45 minutes for the passage from the Formby Lightfloat to the Bar Lightship, always a notorious stretch of water, and her log records: *'Very heavy broken sea, fierce rain and sleet squalls. Vessel pitching and pounding heavily, shipping much water at times.'* Because of the radio silence imposed on account of the PRINCESS VICTORIA disaster, the KING ORRY was unable to make contact with the company at Douglas and advise her position. Many people still recall that day, standing on Douglas Head, eyes focussed on the horizon in the gathering gloom and later the darkness, willing the steamer to make port safely. In the event, the KING ORRY berthed at the Victoria Pier at Douglas at 21.55, exactly eleven hours after leaving Liverpool.

Wednesday, 27th January 1954

With severe east-south-east gales persisting and making Douglas harbour unapproachable, the KING ORRY sailed for the first time in her career direct from Liverpool to Peel on the sheltered west coast of the Isle of Man. She left Liverpool at 10.50 and was alongside Peel breakwater at 15.56 (5 hours 06 minutes). Leaving Peel at 09.55 the next morning, the KING ORRY met the full force of the east-south-east force 9 after rounding the Chicken Rock, and made the passage to Liverpool in 5 hours 48 minutes.

Christmas 1956

With the Christmas traffic building up, fog caused disruption on Friday, 21st December. Some 300 passengers were stranded on board at Liverpool and it was not until 03.45 on Saturday, 22nd December that the KING ORRY was able to sail. Christmas Eve brought a south-easterly force 8 gale and the KING ORRY was diverted to Peel where she arrived at the breakwater at 17.10. There was no rest for the ship over Christmas as the gale increased to force 9, and the MANXMAN needed to berth on the overnight sailing from Liverpool. There is only room for one ship alongside Peel breakwater and at 09.42 on Christmas morning the KING ORRY moved to an anchorage in Peel Bay to allow the MANXMAN in. Blizzard conditions persisted throughout the day and visibility was reported in the log as being 'nil'. On Boxing Day morning the KING ORRY sailed round to Douglas and left for Liverpool at 10.02 with 160 passengers.

Tuesday, 13th January 1959

The KING ORRY left Douglas as usual at 09.02 in an easterly force 2 and smooth sea. At 11.55, owing to dense fog, she anchored one mile off the Bar Lightship and remained there for the next 20 hours. Her master, Captain Lyndhurst Callow, reported that at times he could not see the water from the bridge. The following morning, Wednesday 14th January, the anchor was weighed at 08.18 and an attempt was made to move up the sea channels to Liverpool, but it proved impossible and at 08.38 the anchor was down again. At 11.40 the KING ORRY got underway with the visibility improving and berthed at South Prince's Stage at 13.02, exactly 24 hours late. No attempt was made to sail again to Douglas on 14th January as the fog had settled back on the Mersey, and on the following day the sailing was also cancelled.

Spring 1959

On Tuesday 7th April, Cammell Laird's workforce went on strike and remained out for two-and-a-half months until 24th June. The KING ORRY was trapped in No.4 Drydock and it was not until 2nd July that repair work on her was complete. Because of the strike, she missed the 1959 TT race traffic.

Friday, 26th February 1960

The KING ORRY crossed to Douglas in a south-easterly force 8 and as soon as she had completed discharge she sailed for a sheltered anchorage in Peel Bay, arriving at 18.03. The weather was in fickle mood and by late evening the gale had veered to the south-west. Peel affords no shelter in these conditions and at 22.52 the KING ORRY got underway and sailed north-about to Ramsey Bay. She remained at anchor there from 00.33 until 06.10 and arrived back in Douglas at 07.22. Whilst sheltering from the worst of the winter storms the KING ORRY circumnavigated the Isle of Man far more frequently than she ever did on 'Round the Island' pleasure cruises in the summer.

April and May 1960

During the winter overhaul period a 30ft extension to the bridge deck was built on to the KING ORRY, on each side of the funnel. The company was now required to equip its steamers with liferafts, and the winter steamer carried additional rafts on staging on this extension. The MANXMAN was similarly treated at this time. The effect was to give the KING ORRY the appearance of more top hamper and a much shorter funnel. At this time also, the cravat cowl was removed from her funnel, making her in this respect similar to the 1927-built BEN-MY-CHREE.

Christmas 1961

Dense fog settled down over Merseyside on Wednesday 20th December, and at 10.43 the Seacombe ferry ROYAL DAFFODIL II collided with the KING ORRY's stern on the starboard side, causing extensive damage. Temporary repairs were effected by Cammell Laird. The Steam Packet's winter berth at South Prince's Stage was very vulnerable to this sort of incident and in the previous two years the KING ORRY had been struck by the ferry steamers WALLASEY and BIDSTON in similar conditions.

The morning of Christmas Day saw one of the most serious incidents in the KING ORRY's career. She was scheduled to take the 01.00 sailing from Liverpool, but due to a full easterly gale, this was postponed to 03.00. Despite the conditions she was ordered to approach Douglas and to berth at the Victoria Pier. At 08.10 she was entering the harbour and was between the pier-heads when the gale caught her and she fell very heavily on to the south corner of the pier, splintering her main belting. The old steamer ended 1961 on a very battered note!

Whitsun 1963

The KING ORRY operated the Steam Packet's first ever excursion sailings from Liverpool to Llandudno on 2nd and 3rd June. These sailings were taken over from the Liverpool and North Wales Steamship Company which had ceased operations in September, 1962.

Wednesday, 9th August 1967

The KING ORRY left Liverpool for Douglas at 09.37 with 760 passengers. At 10.18 the chief

Above: KING ORRY in the Crosby Channel on 27th October 1959. *[Raymond Brandreth collection]*

Right: Approaching the old berthing head at Llandudno Pier during Whitsun 1963. The funnel cowl has been removed and a docking bridge added. *[Raymond Brandreth collection]*

Opposite: Two views of KING ORRY at anchor off Seacombe in May 1970. Note the absence of the 'cut-away' or well between numbers 4 and 6 lifeboats. On the KING ORRY this well was only to starboard and in consequence she had to berth starboard side to in order to crane cars on or off. *[John Shepherd collection]*

engineer reported that the main feed pipe had fractured in the boiler and advised the master that it would not be safe to proceed on passage. Accordingly, at 10.30, the KING ORRY swung at the Q.10 buoy and returned to Prince's Stage, arriving back at 11.34. This was the one and only occasion on which she was unable to complete a crossing because of engine trouble.

Sunday, 13th June 1971

The KING ORRY left Douglas at 09.03 with 490 passengers, 16 cars and 180 motorcycles on the last 'shuttle' sailing of TT Week. At 11.19 she received a message to reduce speed as the port of Liverpool was closed to all shipping following a serious leakage of highly volatile chemicals at Bromborough, mid-way between Liverpool and Eastham. Rather than have her return to Douglas, where she would have aggravated an already hectic situation, the KING ORRY was ordered at 12.26 to proceed to Ardrossan, some 200 miles and ten hours' steaming time to the north. The reaction of the passengers to this turn of events is not recorded in the log but the situation at Liverpool improved and, although the upper reaches of the Mersey remained closed, the section from Prince's Stage seawards was re-opened to traffic. At 13.15 the KING ORRY made another 180 degree turn and resumed passage to Liverpool. She arrived at Prince's Stage at 15.07 (6 hours 04 minutes) after the most unusual Douglas to Liverpool passage of her career.

Final summer season 1975

The summer of 1975 turned out to be phenomenally successful for the KING ORRY. The weather was superb throughout and she carried 112,825 passengers, the highest total since 1953. The TT Race Week traffic amounted to 1,939 motorcycles - a total which was exceeded only once before in her career, in 1951.

The KING ORRY operated the annual Tynwald Fair Day excursion on Monday 7th July and took 1,823 Manx people to Llandudno for the day. The Stranraer-Douglas excursion on 27th July was a huge success with 1,630 passengers. On Tuesday 29th July the KING ORRY carried 1,948 passengers from Fleetwood in the morning and sailed back to Llandudno in the afternoon with 2,005. Passenger numbers such as these had not been carried since the early 1950s.

As August wore on it became a time for farewells and the KING ORRY's final passenger sailings took place on Sunday 31st August when she operated the Liverpool-Llandudno excursion with 400 passengers, many of them making the voyage for nostalgic reasons.

Sale and demolition 1976-1979

The KING ORRY was quickly purchased by R.Taylor and Sons of Bury who arranged to have her towed up to Glasson Dock by the tug SEA BRISTOLIAN on 5th November 1975. During the violent westerly gale of 2nd January 1976 the old steamer broke away from the wharf at Glasson Dock and grounded firmly on the top of the spring tide. The KING ORRY was not refloated until 14th April after weeks of work which involved digging away the sand from around her hull. A couple of improbable schemes were dreamt up for her, the first of which was that she would become a detention centre for juvenile offenders berthed at a disused wharf at Millom in the Duddon estuary. Another was that she would be converted into a floating casino - after a facelift the KING ORRY would be based in the North Sea and cater for the oil-rig workers. Not surprisingly, this idea came to nothing.

The KING ORRY was re-sold to Lynch and Son of Rochester, Kent for demolition and was towed round from Glasson Dock by the tug AFON WEN just before Christmas 1977. She lay to buoys at Strood for almost eighteen months before being demolished in 1979.

Opposite bottom: Arriving at Glasson Dock 5th November 1975.

Above and middle: KING ORRY aground at Glasson Dock in 1976. In the upper photograph, daylight is showing for a considerable distance under the bow.

Bottom: At Strood awaiting demolition in September 1978. *[John Shepherd collection]*

Royal Mail Lines' LOMBARDY of 1913. *[Fotoflite incorporating Skyfotos]*

LOMBARDY TO THE WEST INDIES
John B. Hill

Royal Mail Lines will generally be remembered for their elegant passenger liners, which reached their apogee with the attractive ANDES, built in 1939. But the first class passenger service to Brazil and Argentina represented only one aspect of Royal Mail Lines operations. The oldest Royal Mail trade - in fact, the one for which the Royal Charter was granted in 1839 - was to the West Indian islands and until the demise of the company in the 1970s there were always some ships serving the West Indies and nearby Central American and Venezuelan ports. The LOMBARDY was one such ship. Mention is also made of her sister-ship, the SICILY.

Shortly after the Second World War a typical voyage would involve loading a full general cargo in Victoria Dock, London for discharge in Bermuda, Nassau, Jamaica, Curacao and ports in the Lake Maracaibo region of Venezuela (usually Punta Cardon, Bachaquero, Lagunillas, La Salina and San Lorenzo). Cargo would be very varied, with cement, pipes, and machinery for the oil industry stowed in the lower holds; and consumer goods and vehicles for West Indian destinations loaded in the tween decks; not to mention the odd consignment of naval stores for the Royal Navy base at Ireland Island, Bermuda. Homeward bound for London a full cargo was usually available in Jamaica. Bagged sugar would be taken from lighters whilst lying at anchor off Black River, Salt River, and sometimes in Falmouth Harbour. Kingston was generally the final port of call, where holds were topped off with rum, molasses and species. By then the hold ventilators were emitting a quite delightful odour.

Having sailed on several such voyages in 1948-9, I thought some observations about the oldest ship engaged in the trade would be of interest. The LOMBARDY and her sister, the SICILY, had careers lasting 46 and 38 years respectively. Although built for the River Plate trade the LOMBARDY spent many years sailing to the West Indies, and because of her age she had some interesting long-forgotten features.

Both ships were built for David MacIver and Co. by the now long defunct Stockton shipyard, Richardson Duck and Co. and, although these ships traded under the colours of MacIver until 1932, the company had been taken over by Royal Mail in 1919. As LOMBARDY remained with the Group until sold for demolition in 1958, she may hold a record by virtue of being in service with the fleet for 38 years. Although the two ships were built seven years apart, in 1913 and 1920, they were as good as sister-ships. The gap was probably due to the intervention of the First World War. Built on the Isherwood system, with longitudinal framing and a marked degree of tumble-home, the ships were simple 'tween deck freighters

with a deadweight capacity of 6,000 tons. There was accommodation for eight passengers in rooms opening directly onto the dining saloon.

Machinery was very basic, comprising a triple-expansion engine and three Scotch boilers, giving a speed of 12 knots. As was customary in ships of the period, the boilers operated on natural draught, hence the very tall funnel. Electric light was provided by two 30kW steam generators and, unheard of today, the 110 volt supply used the hull structure as an earth return.

The accommodation relied on wind-chutes for ventilation and the officers cabins were fitted with 'compactums' for washing, with a gravity cold water supply from a tank on the boat-deck. In their early days, both ships traded mainly from Liverpool to the River Plate, but latterly LOMBARDY was exclusively on the London-West Indies service.

LOMBARDY holds a particular interest for me as I was her third engineer in 1948 and this experience was something to be remembered. Although the boilers were designed to operate on coal or oil, coal burning was not discarded until 1948. Understandably the change to burning oil in the 28-year-old boilers was not without its problems. I recall passing through King George V Lock, London, bound for the West Indies, with water running out of the boiler ash-pit door and many days were spent on planks and wet sacks, in the 'back ends' expanding leaking boiler tubes.

Although the boilers did not take kindly to the change from coal to oil firing, the firemen certainly did. Following conversion at South Shields, LOMBARDY signed on a complement of Tyneside firemen, who had previously only known coal-fired colliers. They viewed the change from shovelling coal to operating valves controlling the oil flow to the furnaces as almost too good to be true - particularly as the rate of pay was the same.

Another peculiarity of LOMBARDY was that she would only steam with at least two degrees list to port. This was to ensure adequate lubrication of the main engine piston guide plates, which were cracked and could not be cooled in the usual way with cold water. Should the prescribed port list not be maintained, early warning was soon given in the form of sparks coming from the guide bars!

The chief engineer (Sam Beeching in my day) lived in luxury in one of the old passenger cabins adjacent to the saloon, but the other engineers were in cabins beside the engine-room casing. These opened on to a steel deck and the door sills were about 18 inches high to prevent any sea water which accumulated in the passage from entering the cabins. Mine was directly opposite the engine-room door and the steam steering engine was just inside this door.

The rudder was actuated by rods and chains which ran down the passage and along the after deck and the frequent rattle of the steering engine, especially in heavy weather, was something one had to accept in the adjacent cabins.

In 1948 deck and engine-room ratings were still living in the forecastle in two large rooms, sailors to starboard and firemen to port. There was no running water in the forecastle and hot water came from a galvanised boiler, kept permanently on the coal-fired galley range. I assume there were some improvements to these facilities before LOMBARDY went to the breakers in Hong Kong in 1958.

Turning briefly to SICILY, after 20 years with MacIver she was sold to Greek owners in 1933 when the shipping depression was at its worst and fetched only £5,200. Four years later she came under French ownership, and in 1939 suffered the unusual fate of being captured by the Spanish Navy during the Spanish Civil War. She remained under the Spanish flag for 20 years, and during this time she was scuttled, on fire, in Bilbao in 1944 and then rebuilt with new machinery in 1945. As ANTARTICO the 46-year old vessel was wrecked off Santander as she was entering port from Lobito with a cargo of manganese ore on 6th October 1959.

Today few vessels remain in service for half as long as the SICILY. Surely some credit must go to the quality of British shipbuilding earlier this century and to the Isherwood system of construction.

LOMBARDY in the Thames (top) and bunkering at the oil berth in the huge natural harbour at Kingston, Jamaica (bottom). *[Top: V.H. Young and L.A. Sawyer]*

PUTTING THE RECORD STRAIGHT

Letters, additions, amendments and photographs relating to articles in any issues of *Record* are welcomed. Letters may be lightly edited.

Inside Trader

How nice it was to see, in *Record* 9, such an excellent pictorial history of Trader Navigation, particularly since this company was almost a permanent fixture during the first ten or so years I spent in the William Pickersgill/Austin and Pickersgill design and estimating offices. The WELSH TRADER (2) had been completed just before I joined the company, but discussions on building the larger SUSSEX TRADER (2) were just beginning. From then on it was rare not to have some Trader project in hand, even if it was just converting one of the open shelter deckers to a closed configuration.

Later, after he retired, I developed a friendship with Charles Godwin, Managing Director of Trader. It was he who compiled a fleet list which was published in *Marine News* many years ago. He also wrote a series of articles on the operation of a small tramp shipping company (i.e. Trader) published during 1971 in issues 44 to 46 of *Sea Chest*, the journal of the Tyneside Branch of the World Ship Society. According to Mr Godwin, despite the fact that their ultimate owner, Bunge, was chartering in many ships each day for their grain business, they still felt it advisable to have a few ships of their own in order to fulfil grain sales to and from ports which other owners were not keen to use, and formed Trader as a consequence. Before the bulk carriers came along, Trader's aim was always to get maximum deadweight and particularly cubic capacity on a maximum draft of 29 feet and a speed of around 14 knots from their shelter deckers. Even at that draught, Mr. Godwin noted that a company ship bound for the mills in London's Victoria Docks had to lighten first in Royal Albert Dock.

Except for the last, all Trader ships were geared. This was because many of the ports they used at that time did not have shore grain loading facilities and, of course, the gear was a useful adjunct when non-grain back-haul cargoes were carried, and when time charters were fixed to liner companies.

Trader's long assocation with Pickersgills was typical of many built up between builder and owner. In this case it owed much, according to Mr. Godwin, to the first impression generated when the General Manager of William Pickersgill, Fred Hopper, made a cold call on Trader about the time they were looking to build what eventually became WELSH TRADER (2). Fred Hopper was also an accomplished artist and water colourist, and his eye for fine lines and aesthetic appearance was evident in the Pickersgill ships of the era, and not least in WELSH TRADER. Whether she was economical to work is another matter! Although much the same layout was retained for the four subsequent shelter deckers, many of the external frills had been discarded even before new production methods began to be introduced at the yard.

Austin and Pickersgill now had a new shipbuilding complex dedicated to prefabrication, and although SUSSEX TRADER (2) and ESSEX TRADER (2) were basically sisters, the latter was the first ship to be built on the new berths in what had previously been the company's West Yard, but was now the only construction area in the new shipyard, and her design incorporated many new features. Although not evident in your photograph, she had straight-line sheer and camber, and extensive welding. Trader's horror at the possibility of having to accept swedged-sided, block deckhouses, and the elimination of teak work and other frills, led to the yard retaining some of these features in subsequent newbuildings for their good friends, except the last, by when Mr. Godwin had retired.

As with most builders, Pickersgills generally developed their designs from previous newbuildings, and SUSSEX TRADER (2) and ESSEX TRADER (2) could trace their pedigree back to FRAMLINGTON COURT

The Pickersgill-built FRAMLINGTON COURT 5,754/1952) (see Inside Trader) was sold, like many other Court Line motor vessels, including ERRINGTON COURT, to the Jayanti Shipping Co. Ltd. of Bombay, becoming LAXMI JAYANTI in 1962. Greek owners bought her and renamed her SPYROS in 1970, but on 15th May 1973 she sank in the Bay of Bengal after developing leaks.

The motor vessel STANWEAR (8,108/1956) (see Inside Trader) was one of the last ships built for J.A. Billmeir's Stanhope Steamship Co. Ltd. Becoming LADY ERA in 1966, she was sold to Greek owners in 1968, and was wrecked off Port Cartier on 1st February 1977.

(5,754/1952). Although this ship was five feet shorter, beam, depth and draught were almost identical, and one can list REYNOLDS (6,247/1953), the three Larrinaga sisters, plus DARTWOOD (6,139/1956), STANWEAR (8,108/1956), and ERRINGTON COURT (8,176/1957), as coming from the same scrieve. Four Hogarths and GLANELY (8,261/1960) were, like the Trader ships, given the longer length.

Austin and Pickersgill were now trying to develop their standard series principle, and the Trader bulkers were all quickly added to the company's portfolio of standard designs. Thus, SCOTTISH TRADER (3) became the B16 design, and MIDDLESEX TRADER (2), SURREY TRADER and ESSEX TRADER (3) the B20. However, only SCOTTISH TRADER had a sister, Dalgleish's TAMWORTH (11,126/1968) being a prefabricated version.

In line with their demand for high cubic capacity, the Trader bulkers had a somewhat novel layout in that the topside wing tanks were eliminated to give more cargo space. Retaining strength, and satisfying the all-important grain stability regulations, necessitated fitting a centreline bulkhead in some holds: not the ideal arrangement in a bulk carrier. Most bulkers had topside tanks and used them to carry grain cargoes, thereby providing a greater capacity. But this made loading and unloading slower and more labour-intensive, since tanks had to be dried out after use for ballast, and thoroughly cleaned after use for grain so that none was left to clog the pumps.

Your note that ESSEX TRADER (3) differed from her two sisters only with regard to choice of machinery, misses out the fact that she was gearless, and featured all the then attributes of the Austin and Pickersgill standard designs: straight line sheer and camber, and block deckhouse without frills and incorporating swedged stiffening.

Incidentally, there was some controversy over the building of the first pair of 20,000 ton bulk carriers, brought about by the take-over of Austin and Pickersgill by London and Overseas Freighters. Trader had a gentlemen's agreement covering the building of these vessels, although no papers had been signed. Following the take-over, Basil Mavroleon claimed all uncommitted berths for a series of seven or eight, 16,000 ton deadweight, high-class cargo liners for London and Overseas, Mavroleon Brothers, Chandris, and Rethymnis and Kulukundis, and all arrangements with Trader were cancelled. Trader were outraged at this treatment, and it took a lot of urgent and acrimonious argument to revert to the status quo. Needless to say, perceived changes in the market meant that Mavroleon's ships were never built!

Trader Navigation still exists, albeit with new owners. Over the years its name has changed to Trader Navigation Agencies Ltd., and its office at Windsor manages a fleet of some 17 tankers.
JOHN LINGWOOD, 52 Nursery Road, Sunderland SR3 1NT.

Two Bs or not two Bs?
Trader Navigation was a fascinating fleet, and the feature on them is very welcome indeed. Surely, though, the MIDDLESEX and ESSEX TRADERS weren't anything to do with the 'B'-type design? By this I presume is meant the 'PF(B)' type, those strange beasts with the huge number 3 hatch between bridge and funnel, and no sheer except at extreme bow and stern - I would think of the likes of the CLAN ANGUS and CLAN MACKELLAR, or the MANDASOR. The two Trader ships were members of a class of 17 built by Thompsons, yard nos. 611-624 and 626-628. Another example would be the CLAN ALPINE of paddyfield fame - which I've never been able to tell apart from the first type of 'Forts'. The latter were, indeed, known as the 'North Sands'-type, and I've always assumed that they, and the 'Oceans', were built to the Thompson design in question, although for some reason the DORINGTON COURT of 1938 is always mentioned in this context. I've never understood why this should be, as she doesn't bear much resemblance to the North American ships, having, for instance, a very prominent forecastle. I've long had something of an obsession with these Thompson tramps, so it was a nice bonus to get - as well as the two Traders - pictures of the EMPIRE ISEULT, another of their sisters, as the FRANS VAN MIERIS and FARMSUM. Keep those *Records* coming!
CHRISTY MACHALE, 142 Moscow Drive, Liverpool L13 7DL

MECCA vs. FREMANTLE STAR
The LADY RODNEY, mentioned on page 64 of *Record* 9, became the Egyptian MECCA, and ended her seagoing life in 1965 when she rammed the FREMANTLE STAR (8,403/1960) in the southern end of the Gulf of Suez. The FREMANTLE STAR was in the unusual and (her people considered) fortunate situation of having under tow the INDIAN MERCHANT (7,659/1944), a steamer which had broken down in the Red Sea and which the FREMANTLE STAR, homeward bound from Australia with the season's apples, had taken in tow.

Proceeding into the Gulf of Suez during the morning watch, fine weather, calm sea, about 0700 hours, the MECCA was seen heading down from the Canal on a reciprocal course, which would take both ships well clear

The FREMANTLE STAR (8,403/1960) was built by Cammell Laird for Blue Star, and survived the usual transfers around the Vestey group with her identity unchanged. After 20 years' service she was renamed CATARINA, probably for a single voyage east, and arrived at Kaohsiung to be broken up in November 1979.

of each other, port to port. Then, to the amazement of the FREMANTLE STAR's chief officer on the bridge, the MECCA suddenly turned to port and rammed the Blue Star liner forward of the bridge, in way of number 3 hatch. Just before the collision the MECCA's officer-of-the-watch was seen running onto the bridge, tucking in his shirt. He had, it transpired, just nipped down to the toilet leaving only his quartermaster on the bridge, steering. Out of the corner of his eye the quartermaster had seen the FREMANTLE STAR and for reasons best known to himself, hurriedly put his wheel hard a'port ... The Egyptian captain appeared on his bridge, wanting to go astern and pull his ship out of the deep gash he had cut in the FREMANTLE STAR's side, but fortunately Captain Harry Windle dissuaded him from doing this until soundings of his ship's tanks and bilges had been taken and damage assessed - to ensure the ship would not sink when the MECCA withdrew.

Fortunately the INDIAN MERCHANT's boilers were by this time repaired sufficiently for her to let go the tow - she had narrowly missed running up the FREMANTLE STAR's stern. Her master took photos of all that was happening from just before the moment of collision, and these provided useful evidence at the subsequent inquiries. The Indian ship was able to steam into an anchorage, therefore the FREMANTLE STAR's people did earn some salvage money - though not so much as if they had been able to tow her all the way to Suez. When she arrived at the Canal apples from her cargo were spilling out of the gash, to be picked up gleefully by the hordes of small boats crowding alongside. The subsequent Egyptian inquiry held both ships to blame for the collision, but the British inquiry exonerated the FREMANTLE STAR completely.

The FREMANTLE STAR was the first Blue Star liner to be given deck cranes instead of derricks, and also the first to be fitted with hydraulic steel hatch covers. She was drydocked and repaired at Port Said, to resume her normal trading for another 14 years. The MECCA was beached at Port Said and became one of those vessels placed to block the Canal after the Six Days War of 1967. I last saw her in 1977, clear of the Canal but still on the beach, and still with the gash in her bow caused when she cut into the FREMANTLE STAR.

Immediately after this dramatic voyage, the FREMANTLE STAR's master, Captain Windle, was promoted to Marine Superintendent while his chief officer, Bill Askew, was promoted to master.
CAPTAIN A.W. KINGHORN, 15 Kendal Avenue, Cullercoats, North Shields, Tyne and Wear NE30 3AQ.

The response to Peter Newall's article on pilgrim ships has been very gratifying, and we intend to publish the
additional submissions as a follow-up feature in the next issue.

BAIKAL's Bolshevik end
In my article on the BAIKAL in *Record* 5, I wrote that I had been unable to determine the details of her final fate. Now, thanks to Edward Wilson of Burntisland in Fife, I can complete the story. Edward, who is somewhat of an expert on Tsarist and Soviet shipping, brought to my attention an article which appeared recently in a German magazine and describes the ship's end. It seems that during the Russian Civil War the BAIKAL was in Bolshevik hands. Whilst engaged in carrying ammunition she was attacked off Listvyanka by SIBIRJAK, a White Russian tug which was fitted with a gun. The BAIKAL was soon hit and set on fire. She was hastily abandoned by her crew, and shortly afterwards blew up and sank. During more peaceful times the wreck was raised and scrapped.
COLIN TURNER, 86 Riverside Drive, Stoneclough, Radcliffe, M26 1HY.

Back to Barrow
Concerning the photograph of Barrow (page 176, *Record* 7 and page 53, *Record* 9) I cannot support either of Ken Royall's suggested identifications for vessel (1). I stick with my original suggestion for the following reasons:

1. AFFLECK's stern, although not blown off, was buckled upwards with the main area of damage on the port quarter. As can be seen in the photograph the ship still has its two stern depth charge chutes indicating that very little of the quarterdeck has been destroyed.

2. The REDMILL suffered very similar damage to the AFFLECK. Her upper deck was buckled whilst the decks below were blown off as far forward as frame 147. However, she was moved from Londonderry to Belfast before being towed to Barrow and is known to have been in Belfast in September and October 1945. She was officially listed as joining the Reserve at Barrow on 7th December 1945.

3. She cannot possibly be the MANNERS for two reasons. Firstly, the vessel is clearly one of the turbo-electric frigates and the MANNERS was one of the much shorter diesel electric types. Secondly, the MANNERS was torpedoed by U 1051. (Admiralty Historical Branch Research in 1992 concluded that U 1051 had attacked MANNERS and had been sunk in counter-attacks by the AYLMER, CALDER and BENTINCK. U 1172 was sunk by KEATS, TYLER and BLIGH on the following day, 27th January 1945.) The MANNERS was hit twice, the first strike was right aft and put the propellors out of action. The second hit was about 25 feet from the stern and the

entire aft section of the ship was blown off, reducing her length by about one third, and causing 43 deaths and 14 wounded.

I noticed three minor errors in *Record* 9. The caption to the DZIERZYNSKI on page 27 is incomplete *(It should read '... had been spent on the bottom of the Baltic.' Ed.)* On page 54, divers reported on the hull of BARON VERNON on 29th May, not 29th March. And the first sentence on page 55 should begin 'The BARON VERNON' rather than 'BARON DUNMORE'.

Finally, can someone, somewhere, positively identify the Captain Class frigate and the elusive merchant ship in *Record* 9, page 53?
BOB TODD, Head, Historic Photographs and Ship Plans Section, National Maritime Museum, Greenwich, London SE10 9NF. http://www.nmm.ac.uk
Ken Royall concurs with Bob's identification. He suggests the bucket dredger (number 11 on the photograph on page 53) is the PIEL (1,226/1927).

Matters arising from *Record* 8
Both the STRATHNAVER and STRATHAIRD retained their three funnels throughout the Second World War (page 239 of *Record* 8). I have before me a photograph of STRATHAIRD taken on 10th October 1946 in the Palmers' Hebburn graving dock and she still has three funnels. The photograph of MONARCH OF BERMUDA shows her at Southampton during rebuilding by John I. Thornycroft and Co. Ltd., and we have a note that she was on Berth 40, Test Quay for the duration. And one small discrepancy concerning LA MARGUERITE (page 251): you record that her last excursion was on 28th September 1925, yet she sailed for the breakers several days earlier, on the 22nd!
DAVID HODGE, National Maritime Museum, Greenwich, London SE10 9NF. http://www.nmm.ac.uk
[LA MARGUERITE sailed for the breakers on 22nd October 1925. Ed.]

As well as re-engining SUD AMERICANO and SUD EXPRESO, Norddeutscher Lloyd also lengthened them - see the new raked bow and forecastle in both photos on pages 200-1. I have two additional two-funnelled ships, the Glen Line's GLENOGLE of 1882 and Skinner's STIRLING CASTLE of the same year. I believe both are properly classed as cargo liners as I do not think passenger accommodation was added to the STIRLING CASTLE until after her sale to the Italians. *[Can anyone offer photos? Ed.]*

The low pressure turbines in RANCHI (The Coaly Tyne, page 239) were a later addition in 1930; the original machinery was just the reciprocators. There is nothing unusual about her being registered at Newcastle. It was the standard P&O practice from about the 1870s to the end of the 1920s to register their ships in the port where they were built - hence many ships were registered at Greenock and Belfast as well as Newcastle.

Apart from some wartime voyages, DOMINION MONARCH never 'went homeward across the Pacific via the Panama Canal' (page 240). Both her outward and homeward peacetime voyages were always made via Cape Town.

Both the MONARCH and QUEEN OF BERMUDA were ordered from Vickers' Barrow yard but the contract for the MONARCH was re-allocated to Walker to relieve unemployment. The QUEEN was built at Barrow, not Walker (page 241).

Ritson's funnel was not blue and white striped (page 243). The stripes were black, but the funnel is more usually described as black with four thin white stripes.

The explanation of the 'two tubular struts' on DUNKERY BEACON (page 250) is very simple. To quote: 'To keep the port side of the forward deck clear for launching the aircraft, her builders stayed the foremast by a tripod'. This feature remained with the ship post war.
BILL LAXON, Waimarana, Upper Whangateau Road, PO Box 171, Matakana 1240, New Zealand.
Thanks also to Brian Walker of Kaikoura, New Zealand for correcting DOMINION MONARCH's itinerary. Ed.

BARTON (*Record* 8 page 235) was not broken up, but was wrecked on 13th March 1936. The February 1995 and May 1998 issues of *Tees Packet* relate how the Waterman steamer WEST HIKA (5,372/1919) ran aground in fog three miles south of Seaham Harbour on 15th January 1936. She resisted all efforts at refloating, and was sold at the end of February to the South Stockton Shipbreaking Co. Ltd., who hoped to salvage her and take her to their yard at Thornaby, the former Richardson Duck shipyard. BARTON had been bought by them for scrapping on 18th February, but was pressed into service on the WEST HIKA. Unfortunately, she struck the steamer on 14th March and promptly sank alongside. BARTON was not salvaged, although WEST HIKA was some six months later, ending her days at Blyth after frustrated attempts to get her back into commercial service.

PEARL HAVEN (page 215) had one more intermediate name between EVANGELISMOS and CHIOS: she was ANGLIA of Mansion Investment Co. of Limassol from 1975 to 1976.

LOCHSIDE II (page 237) did not become SIRIUS, but ARMOR of Sirius Compania Naviera, Honduras in 1972. But the plot thickens. Her arrest in May 1975 was reported in *Marine News* June 1976 (page 236), then sailing Brest for breakers at Morlaix on 5th May 1976, but the August 1976 issue (page 316) reports her as having left Limassol for Jounieh on 26th June 1976. The next mention is in August 1977 (page 386), when she again is reported sold by Sirius Compania Naviera and arrives at Monsigny et Fils, Morlaix for breaking in June 1977. So did she get a reprieve and extra voyage, and why was she arrested in the first instance?

I have a yard number 977 for AMSTERDAM (page 247), so this immediately preceded the series allocated for the SCOTTISH tankers.

K. RAPANOS (page 260) became PENELOPE when sold to the Italians in 1952: a much safer name!
GEORGE ROBINSON, 7 Hornbeam Walk, Cottingham, East Yorkshire HU16 4RS.

LUCY gets a diesel
I was interested to see your article British Yard, Greek Tramp in *Record* 8, and especially the photograph and caption showing the motorship LUCY. The ship was, in fact, originally a steamer, having been built with a triple-expansion engine with a Bauer-Wach exhaust turbine. After three years trading with this machinery, which was installed with first cost, simplicity and reliability as the primary considerations, it became apparent that for her to compete successfully in the freight market, a different means of propulsion with a reduced fuel consumption was necessary.

The LUCY was therefore returned to her builders for re-engining with a three-cylinder, Gray-Doxford opposed-piston, two-stroke, oil engine developing 3,300 BHP. She arrived at West Hartlepool on 23rd October 1960 and the work took 115 days. I was working for the Journal of Commerce at the time and was sent to attend the trial trip. This took place on 14th February 1961 and LUCY then sailed on her first voyage with her new engine, for Cuba via Rotterdam.
CRAIG J.M. CARTER, 15 King's Court, Well Lane, Higher Bebington, Wirral, Merseyside CH63 8QL.